LIST OF PUBLICATIONS

AMERICANA

ADAMS, HENRY. *Esther, A Novel* (1884)................ $3.50
ALLEN, ETHAN. *Reason the only oracle of man* (1784).... $5.00
BROWN, CHARLES BROCKDEN. *Uncollected Writings*........ $3.00
EMERSON, RALPH WALDO. *Nature* (1836)............... $3.50
FRENEAU, PHILIP. *Letters on Various Subjects* (1799).... $4.00
GOMARA, FRANCISCO LOPEZ DE. *The Pleasant historie of the Weast India atchieved by H. Cortes* (1578)........ $5.00
GRAY, R. *A Good Speed to Virginia* (1609); (*with R. RICH. Newes from Virginia*)............................. $2.00
JEFFERSON, THOMAS. *The Rights of British America* (1774) $2.00
MORTON, NATHANIEL. *New Englands Memoriall* (1669).. $4.00
POE, EDGAR ALLAN. *Letters and Documents*............... $3.00
WASHINGTON, GEORGE. *Journal* (1754).................. $1.50
WHITAKER, ALEXANDER. *Good Newes from Virginia* (1613) $2.00
WILMER, LAMBERT A. *Merlin; and, Recollections of E. A. Poe* (1827) $1.50

ENGLISH

An Herbal (1525) $3.50
BLENERHASSET, THOMAS. *A Revelation of Minerva* (1582) $3.00
BRINSLEY, JOHN. *A Consolation for our Grammar Schooles* (1622) $3.50
CAIUS, JOHN. *A Boke of . . . the . . . Sweatyng Sicknesse* (1552) $2.50
CAMPION, EDMUND, *Historie of Ireland* (c. 1571) $4.50
CECIL, WILLIAM. *The Execution of Justice in England* (1583) $2.00
ELYOT, SIR THOMAS. *The Castel of Helth* (1541)........ $4.00
GRANGE, JOHN. *The Golden Aphroditis* and *Granges Garden of Verse* (1577) $3.00
HENRY THE MINSTREL. *Actis & Deidis of . . . Schir William Wallace* (1570) $5.00
HEYWOOD, THOMAS. *An Apology for Actors* (1612). Bound with I. G., *A Refutation of the Apology* (1615)...... $4.50
JOURDAIN, SILVESTER. *A discovery of the Barmudas, otherwise called the Isle of Divels* (1610).............. $2.00
NICCOLS, RICHARD. *The Beggers Ape* (1623)............ $1.50
SPAGNUOLI, BAPTISTA (MANTUANUS). *The Eglogs* (1567) $4.00
TURNER, WILLIAM. *A Book of the Natures of all Wines* (1568) $4.00
VAN DER NOOT, JAN. *A Theatre for Voluptuous Worldlings* (1569) $5.00

THE LAY PREACHER

by

JOSEPH DENNIE

Edited

WITH AN INTRODUCTION

And

A BIBLIOGRAPHICAL NOTE

by

MILTON ELLIS

Professor of English, University of Maine

SCHOLARS' FACSIMILES & REPRINTS
103 Park Avenue
New York
1943

INTRODUCTION

Joseph Dennie (1768-1812), "the ornament to society, the Columbus of polite literature in this hemisphere, the zealous friend, and the elegant writer," as a successor in the editorship of the *Port Folio* magazine described him, was the ablest writer of familiar essays in the United States before Washington Irving. His American reputation in his own time was great. President Timothy Dwight styled him "the Addison of America." The young Irving visited him, based his Launcelot Langstaff partly upon him,[1] and was probably influenced in his early work by the contemporary popularity of the *Lay Preacher* essays. A generation later, Nathaniel Hawthorne referred to him as "once esteemed the finest writer in America." The Federalist statesmen in the waning years of the Adams administration invited him to the capital as a literary ally; and as editor of the *Port Folio* from 1801 to his death in 1812, he was the chief arbiter of literary taste in the country. The Englishman William Cobbett solicited the publication of the *Lay Preacher* in London; and Thomas Moore, visiting in Philadelphia, praised Dennie as one of the "sacred few" whom

'Twas bliss to live with, and 'twas pain to leave.

This fame as a writer rested mainly upon the *Lay Preacher* essays, written between 1795 and 1801, of which the two small collections published in 1796 and 1817 are here reprinted. The first essay appeared in the *Farmer's Weekly Museum*, at Walpole, New Hampshire, on October 13, 1795, and the last in Joseph T. Buckingham's *New England Galaxy*, July 10, 1818, eight years after the author's death. Of the one hundred and seventeen essays, ninety were first printed in the *Farmer's Museum*, thirteen in the *Gazette of the United States*, at Philadelphia, eleven in the *Port Folio*, at Philadelphia, one in the *Eagle: or Dartmouth Centinel*, at Hanover, New Hampshire, one in the *New England Galaxy*, at Boston, and one as a separate leaflet in Philadelphia, in 1818.

Previously, Dennie had contributed the *Farrago* series of twenty-five light personal essays to Vermont and New Hampshire papers and to his own short-lived periodical venture, the *Tablet*, May 19 to August 11, 1795. In the following autumn he moved to Walpole, where David Carlisle, Jr., a former apprentice of Isaiah Thomas, was carrying on an enterprising newspaper, *The New Hampshire Journal: Or The Farmer's Weekly Museum*. To this Dennie had already contributed the first number and perhaps others of a series called "The Saunterer," designed to be produced in collaboration with Royall Tyler and others.

---

[1]Pierre M. Irving, *Life and Letters of Washington Irving* (New York, 1869), I, 155.

INTRODUCTION

The beginning of the *Lay Preacher* is thus described in a letter Dennie wrote to his mother on April 26, 1797:[2]

> . . . There was a press here conducted by a young man, honest, industrious, and then a partner of Thomas. I determined, by the agency of my pen, to convince him that I could be useful, and then—my humble knowledge of human agency taught me—I was sure he would encourage me when his own *interest* was the prompter. Without saying a word respecting a stipend, I wrote and gave him an essay on *Wine and New Wine,* and called it the *Lay Preacher.* It had been objected to my earliest compositions [the *Farrago* essays] that they had been sprightly rather than moral. Accordingly, I thought I would attempt to be useful, by exhibiting truths in a plain dress to the common people.

The title and character of the *Lay Preacher* had their origin partly in Dennie's admiration of the "Shandean" *Sermons of Yorick* of Lawrence Sterne, and partly in his own experience as lay reader in the Episcopal church at Claremont, New Hampshire, during the fall and winter of 1793-94, which almost induced him to become a clergyman.[3] The combination of moralist and essayist was one eminently suited to his character and temperament. "As a preacher he could appropriately censure the follies, crudities, and shortcomings of his countrymen; as a *lay* preacher he was not debarred from rambling into politics, literature, and occasionally frivolous satire on manners and society."[4] Each essay was headed by a text from Scripture, and followed the general outline of a sermon in little. The range of subjects treated was extensive, including the inculcation of homely virtues, the pleasures of a simple and retired life, stories of Biblical characters, discussions of literature, and warnings against the influence of Jacobinical philosophies in American politics. In the decades before the appearance of Irving and the *Salmagundi* group, the *Lay Preacher* essays won a wide hearing and were reprinted in newspapers and magazines throughout the country.

---

[2]*The Letters of Joseph Dennie,* edited by Laura G. Pedder (University of Maine Studies, Second Series, No. 36, Orono, 1936), 158.

[3]For a more extended account of this experience see [Harold] Milton Ellis, *Joseph Dennie and His Circle* (University of Texas Studies in English No. 3, Austin, 1915), 54-57.

[4]*Ibid.,* 88-89.

INTRODUCTION

The series continued in the *Farmer's Museum* without a break from October 12, 1795, to May 24, 1796; irregularly from then until midsummer of 1797; and at longer intervals thereafter until August 26, 1799. In the autumn of that year Dennie became a contributor to and subsequently literary editor of the *Gazette of the United States*, the official Federalist organ, published at Philadelphia. To this periodical he contributed a series called the "Lay Preacher of Pennsylvania," which ran irregularly from November 8, 1799 to March 15, 1800. This series, never specifically acknowledged by Dennie, is identified as his by the inclusion, on December 30, of his essay "Motherhood: The Story of Hagar,"[5] which had appeared the year before in the *Farmer's Museum*. A number of older *Lay Preacher* essays were also reprinted, often in a considerably edited and revised form, in the *Gazette;* and the greater number reappeared in the *Port Folio*, from 1801 to 1808. For this publication he wrote a new introductory essay, "Go about the Streets," printed January 17, 1801. On December 12, 1807, a new sequence began and continued without interruption until February 13, 1808. These were probably not freshly written but taken from "a file of unpublished Lay Preachers" which he had asked his friend Roger Vose to forward from Walpole, New Hampshire, "by the earliest Mail," on February 7, 1800.[6] Some others were probably left at his death, since in 1818 Buckingham printed one, and an unsuccessful beginning of a series in separate pamphlets was begun at Philadelphia in the same year.

Dennie's ambitious hopes for the publication of his essays in book form in England and America were mostly doomed to disappointment, and the one collection issued during his lifetime brought him no financial reward. This was *The Lay Preacher, or Short Sermons for Idle Readers*, published by Carlisle at Walpole, in August, 1796.

The volume was well received, especially by the Federalist press and clergy, who praised it as much for its correct religious and political sentiments as for its literary qualities. It also enjoyed a moderate sale, but one of several business failures of his publisher, Dennie reported, deprived him of his "whole property in the sale of my little book."[7] Upon it his literary reputation had to rest during his lifetime. Since it included only thirty-eight of the essays, he realized that this was a slight basis

---

[5]The title is mine. See *Joseph Dennie and His Circle,* 112-113 and 243-244; also *Gazette of the United States,* December 12, 1799.

[6]*Letters,* 178.

[7]*Letters,* 171.

for fame, and several times made plans for the publication of the whole series. In May, 1798, the issuance of a "new and elegant edition of the *Lay Preacher*, with very copious additions" was forecast by the *Farmer's Museum*. Then Cobbett ("Peter Porcupine") promised to publish the essays in Philadelphia and pay $1000 for the copyright, but this plan fell through when Cobbett left America after losing his lawsuit to Dr. Benjamin Rush. In April, 1800, the *Gazette of the United States* issued proposals for an edition in two volumes, royal octavo, to be published by subscription at a price of four dollars. When the *Port Folio* was established in 1801, an edition was still discussed, but soon the hope must have faded into a mirage.

In 1816, four years after Dennie's death, John E. Hall, having come into possession of his literary papers, projected a biography of the essayist and an edition of his works. Only an experimental collection of twenty-eight *Lay Preacher* essays actually saw the light. The edition was restricted to a few impressions, with the implication that more would follow if it were well received.[8] By then, however, the earlier volume was already becoming a rarity, and the great popularity of Irving's *Sketch Book*, appearing so soon afterward, cast the new book completely into the shade. The *Lay Preacher* series passed gradually into oblivion.

In our edition the eighteenth-century phrasal punctuation and certain archaic spellings like "scholastick" have been modernized, though the English spelling of nouns like "honour," which was a matter of principle with the author, has been retained (the usage is uniform in the 1817 volume, and occasional in the 1796); and Dennie's over-fondness for words and phrases in italics or quotation marks, and proper names in capitals, has been toned down. These alterations have been made in order that superficial eccentricities and irritating differences in typographical usage may not come unnecessarily between the reader and his enjoyment of the author's ideas and expression. Obvious printers' errors have been corrected; otherwise the text stands as it was published. Two essays (the second and the ninth) are omitted from the 1796 edition because they were included in altered form in that of 1817, where they are the eighth and the twenty-eighth respectively. Dennie revised many of his essays with great care for anticipated republication, expanding or pruning with generally sound judgment; it will hence be observed that those in the second volume are usually longer, more polished in style, and maturer in thought.

---

[8]See Hall's Introduction to the 1817 volume, below.

INTRODUCTION

It is hoped that the freshness, fluency, urbanity, and literary flavor of the essays, despite the author's mild affectations, playful vanity, and strong Federalist bias, will prove sufficient justification for reprinting them, since they are no longer generally available for twentieth-century readers. A recent canvass of forty-two of the larger and more prominent University and public libraries in the United States reveals that the 1796 *Lay Preacher* is to be found in only sixteen of them. The 1817 edition is still rarer, being available, so far as known to me, only in the New York Public Library and the libraries of the American Antiquarian Society, the New Hampshire Historical Society, the Library Company of Philadelphia, and Harvard and Princeton Universities. Such a degree of obscurity is not merited by Dennie's real achievement as an essayist and his importance as a pioneer editor and critic.

MILTON ELLIS

Orono, Maine
September, 1942

BIBLIOGRAPHICAL NOTE

The Lay Preacher; or Short Sermons for Idle Readers, printed by David Carlisle, Jr., in 1796, at Walpole, New Hampshire, and "Sold at his Bookstore," was a duodecimo volume with pagination iv, 1 leaf, 6-132 pp. The title page bore the motto " 'Therefore, seeing we have this ministry, we faint not.' St. Paul." The New York Public Library copy was one presented by Isaiah Thomas, the historian of printing in America, to the American Antiquarian Society, and the title page bears his inscription of the gift. The book was sold or given by the Librarian of the Society, Samuel F. Haven, to E. A. Duyckinck and thence came to the New York Public Library as a part of the Duyckinck collection.

The 1817 edition, *The Lay Preacher,* "collected and arranged by J. E. Hall," and printed in Philadelphia by Harrison Hall, is slightly smaller than the earlier one, 24°, and comprises xii + 168 pages. The edition appeared early in 1817, though the Introduction is dated 1816. John Ewing Hall was an early contributor to the *Port Folio,* and after Dennie's death became the fourth editor to carry on in succession his penname "Oliver Oldschool." The essays are introduced by a Preface in which the editor tells of his efforts, including a visit to New England in 1816, to gather material for a projected biography of the author. Harrison Hall, his brother, was printer of the *Port Folio.* Two other brothers, Judge James Hall of Illinois and Thomas Mifflin Hall, as well as their mother, Sarah (Ewing) Hall, were also more or less closely connected with Dennie and the *Port Folio.*

M. E.

TABLE OF CONTENTS
(1796 Edition)

TABLE OF CONTENTS

(1817 Edition)

LAY PREACHER;

OR

SHORT SERMONS,

FOR

IDLE READERS.

"THEREFORE, SEEING WE HAVE THIS MINISTRY—
WE FAINT NOT." St. *PAUL.*

Published according to ACT *of* CONGRESS.

PRINTED AT *WALPOLE,* NEWHAMPSHIRE,
By DAVID CARLISLE, Jun.
And Sold at his BOOKSTORE.

1796.

ADVERTISEMENT

MOST of the following pages originally appeared in the *Farmer's Weekly Museum,* a rural paper of New Hampshire. Surrounded by plain husbandmen rather than by polished scholars, the Author, both in the selection of his subjects and their vehicle, has been more studious of the useful than the brilliant. To instruct the villager was his primary object. Hence, an easy and obvious style was indispensable. To rise to the gorgeous phrase of Bolingbroke would have been absurd; to sink to the vulgarity of L'Estrange would have been ignominious. The familiarity of Franklin's manner, and the simplicity of Sterne's proved most auxiliary to his design. He, therefore, adventured their union. Diffident of success, and prepared for censure, he will not be surprised at a harsh sentence from the critical tribunal. The vanity of authorship has already caused him to prove the negligence of his natal town; the same passion now urges him on to try the suffrages of the country. Should this, like former attempts, slide rapidly down the slope of oblivion, it will add the last item to the catalogue of literary disappointments, and cure

The AUTHOR.

I

"Two are better than one."

THIS is Solomon's theory, and I like it; his practice was rather too extensive, for in his luxurious palace seven hundred wives and three hundred concubines were better than one. Whether the women of Jerusalem were composed of more manageable materials than modern females I am at a loss, for Josephus, whose works I have turned over to gain information on this knotty point, says nothing of the matter. However, I am inclined to think Solomon made his domestic arrangement soon after he "planted vineyards." Had he chosen a graver moment he would not have told the most confidential of his eunuchs that seven hundred expensive wives and three hundred capricious concubines were better than one. Why, the revenues of gold-paved Jerusalem or the bagnios of its suburbs could not have furnished robes for the married dames nor rakes for the free! Men, sage like Solomon, are generally moderate in their arithmetic of pleasures. But this was too bold a sum in multiplication, even for a polygamist to work.

In all probability, Solomon, though the oriental writers expatiate upon his resources, found his stock too scanty for the many and great claims which "the daughters of Jerusalem" must have made. For late in life, when the "pitcher" was broken and the "silver cord" of love loosed and his "desires failed," we find him gravely composing a sententious proverb in praise of sociability and reducing a thousand companions to one. His reasons, too, are not drawn as they would have been when he formed his seraglio, from passion and pleasure, but from utility. For he supports his opinion by arguing, in the context, that "two are better than one," because in difficulty or in battle they mutually assist or, bedded in a frosty night, they keep each other warm.

Although, in remarking upon Solomon's voluptuousness, I have been moved from my natural gravity as a preacher, yet let not the wanton reader construe my sermon as a satire upon the sage prince. After animadverting upon the excess of his practice, it is my intention to echo the benevolence and utility of his social principle.

[5]

"Two are better than one." Dr. Franklin thought so when he recommended early marriages. As I am of singular continence myself, I know nothing of the matter; but St. Paul, an apostle of experience, tells bachelor and virgin Christians that it is better to marry than burn. If they feel this heat, therefore, let them quench it in legal couples and choose for the wedding-ring posy, "two are better than one." My physician declares that, in these degenerate days when illicit love is common, early marriage is favourable to *health;* the philosophers affirm that it is to *morals.* The Preacher therefore concludes that "two are better than one," applied to matrimony, is a precept productive of happiness, and that a young man who will reject *all* the concubines and six hundred and ninety-nine of the wives which Solomon thought necessary, may be pronounced wiser, as it respects women, than that prince.

In the dark ages, as they were justly styled, devotional men used to think that St. Peter, the porter of Heaven's wicket, would not open it but to one at a time. Accordingly, monks and hermits would wander, or reside solitary in deserts and caves, and insist that an error had crept into the Proverbs and that Solomon certainly wrote *"One* is better than *two."* This was a vile interpretation; and if they had meditated their Bibles well they would have discovered that the founder of their religion was never so happy as when "much people" surrounded him, and that the apostles chose companions in their travel; the one sat socially at a wedding supper and the others resorted to the temples, the town hall, and the market place.

I grieve to see a melancholy man moping in the chimney corner, refusing to "eat bread," and when the cup goes round, unwilling to pledge a bumper. Trust me, thou son of spleen, happiness is doubled by participation. Arise, therefore, and be even as this publican; be social, be merry, go to the door of thy tent, and if thou seest a man of understanding pass by, intreat him with a "turn in hither, I beseech thee." So shall the "evil spirit" flee, as of yore, from the harp of the shepherd, and all the cares of thy heart be lulled by the pleasant communion of a friend.

III

"How long wilt thou sleep O sluggard? When wilt thou arise out of thy sleep?"

NOT until you have had another nap, you reply, not until there has been a little more folding of the hands!

Various philosophers and naturalists have attempted to define man. I never was satisfied with their labours. Absurd to pronounce him a two-legged, unfeathered animal, when it is obvious he is a *sleepy* one. In this world there is business enough for every individual. A sparkling sky over his head to admire, a fertile soil under his feet to till, and innumerable objects useful and pleasant to chase. But such in general is the provoking indolence of our species, that the lives of many, if impartially journalized, might be truly said to have consisted of a series of slumbers. Some men are infested with day dreams as well as by visions of the night; they travel a certain insipid round, like the blind horse of the mill, and, as Bolingbroke observes, perhaps beget others to do the like after them. They may sometimes open their eyes a little, but they are soon dimmed by some lazy fog; they may sometimes stretch a limb, but its effort is soon palsied by procrastination. Yawning amid tobacco fumes, they seem to have no hopes except that their bed will soon be made, and no fears except that their slumbers shall be broken by business clamouring at the door.

How tender and affectionate is the reproachful question of Solomon in the text. When wilt thou arise out of thy sleep? The Jewish Prince, whom we know to be an active one from the temple which he erected and from the books he composed, saw, when he cast his eyes around his city, half his subjects asleep. Though in many a wise proverb he had warned them of the baneful effects of indolence, they were deaf to his charming voice and blind to his noble example. The men servants and the maid servants whom he hired, nodded over their domestic duties in the royal kitchen, and when in the vineyards he had planted he looked for grapes, lo, they brought forth *wild* grapes, for the vintager was drowsy.

THE LAY PREACHER

At the present time few Solomons exist to preach against pillows, and never was there more occasion for a sermon. Our country being at peace, not a drum is heard to rouse the slothful. But, though we are exempted from the tumult and vicissitudes of war, we should remember there are many posts of duty, if not of danger, and at these we should vigilantly stand. If we will stretch the hand of exertion, means to acquire competent wealth and honest fame abound; and when such ends are in view how shameful to wilfully close our eyes. He who surveys the paths of active life will find them so numerous and lengthy that he will feel the necessity of early rising and late taking rest, to accomplish so much travel. He who pants for the shade of speculation will find that literature cannot flourish in the bowers of indolence and monkish gloom. Much midnight oil must be consumed and innumerable pages examined by him whose object is to be really wise. Few hours has that man to sleep, and not one to loiter, who has many coffers of wealth to fill or many cells in his memory to store.

Among the various men whom I see in the course of my pilgrimage through this world, I cannot frequently find those who are broad awake. Sloth, a powerful magician, mutters a witching spell, and deluded mortals tamely suffer this drowsy being to bind a fillet over their eyes. All their activity is employed in turning themselves like the door on its rusty hinge, and all the noise they make in this world is a snore. When I see one designed by nature for noble purposes, indolently declining the privilege and heedless, like Esau, bartering the birthright for what is of less worth than his red pottage of lentils, for liberty to sit still and lie quietly, I think I see, not a man but an oyster. The drone in society, like that fish on our shores, might as well be sunken in the mud and inclosed in a shell as stretched on a couch or seated in a chimney corner.

The season is now approaching fast when some of the most plausible excuses for a little more sleep must fail. Enervated by indulgence, the slothful are of all men most impatient of cold, and they deem it never more intense than in the morning. But the last bitter month* has rolled away, and now, could I persuade to the experiment, the sluggard will discover that he may toss off the

---

*February.

[8]

bed quilt and try air of early day without being congealed! He may be assured that sleep is a very stupid employment and differs little from death, except in duration. He may receive it implicitly, upon the faith both of the physician and the Preacher, that morning is friendly to health and the heart, and if the idler is so manacled by the chains of habit that he can, at first, do no more, he will do wisely and well to inhale pure air, to watch the rising sun, and mark the magnificence of nature.

IV

"Neither give place to the devil."

A certain writer, though not a Bishop, has somewhere asserted that the Devil goes about in more pleasing shapes than that of a roaring Lion. It is at those seasons, my readers, when this personage is disguised, or attired in agreeable array, that we should guard against his wiles. If he never assailed us except when clad in that tremendous coat of armour given him by the Calvinistic divines, neither St. Paul nor a more modern moralist would caution you against giving him place. I trow, as my predecessor Daniel Burgess says, if John Bunyan's Devil alone appeared, that to saucer eyes, a cloven foot, and a dragon's tail, not even a hardened sinner would open his gate. But when Satan chooses to walk to and fro in masquerade through the world, his deformities all hidden either by a broad mantle or a flowing robe, then he allures the eye, then he taints the heart.

Now, as we are not ignorant of his devices, and as Moses, an old authentic historian, has apprised us of his subtlety, it may be useful to those who carelessly judge the characters from appearance, to describe some of the most common shapes which the Tempter assumes. Hence, without a very laborious process in reasoning, it may soon be discovered that many of the most common and favorite objects of pursuit are the Devil.

A bag of money, for instance, if we seek it in company with Integrity and Industry, is not only a harmless but useful acquisition. But when Avarice advises to dig, Knavery to undermine, or Ambition to soar for it, the possessor will find a cloven foot in the sack's mouth instead of the cup of Benjamin.

A well-known poet once exclaimed, "Oh, grant me *honest* fame, or grant me none." For this kind of reputation all should be anxious. Without a good name, man would be poor indeed. But when, greedy of applause, we hunt after it in pathless ways at the expense of morals or health; when a drunkard thinks to gain it from an ocean of liquor or a sensualist by keeping three hundred concubines; when a fop imagines it attached to tawdry clothes or a malcontent to subversion of government, in all these cases men are actually striving to give place to the Devil.

[10]

THE LAY PREACHER

When a factious partizan wishes that our liberty should corrupt to licentiousness, when he surveys the administration or reads the speeches of Washington and then has the wickedness and effrontery to pronounce him a Caesar or a Cromwell; when he defames Jay as a dupe and parasite and Hamilton as a stock-jobber, be assured that the moonbeams have glowed intensely on the crazy head of the railer, for he is mad and hath a Devil.

There has lately arisen a new sect in Philosophy, styled Speculators, not very intense thinkers but yet, contradictory as it may seem, absorbed in speculation. Like Locke and other profound metaphysicians, they are more conversant with ideas than with reality. Like an insane beggar who sometimes solicits charity at my door, they are perpetually vaunting of vast possessions in land and muttering about titles, grants, and charters. I have been inclined to think they are allied to the noble families of gypsies and jugglers, from the variety and adroitness of their sleights of hand. I have turned over at least ten different dictionaries to find a definition of the word "Speculation," and after fruitless attempts I am obliged to frame one myself and conclude that it means the sale of a cloud for a valuable consideration. Therefore, as a grave and scriptural author declares Satan to be "the prince of the power of the *air*," we may regularly infer that all transactions of the above nature are within his jurisdiction and that Speculators give place to the Devil.

The fair sex display in general such admirable taste and judgment in the choice of their favorites, it is hardly credible that a being so ungracious and sooty as Satan could find any quarter from their delicacy. But I am assured by a respectable character, well versed in the ways and wiles of women, that when they scold for hours a worthy husband, or display unreasonable caprice and coquetry to a deserving lover, they not only give place to the Devil but frequently prevent his visit, and act the part of the fiend themselves.

[11]

V

"Favor is deceitful"

UNDOUBTEDLY, though Lavater, a Swiss clergyman, whose faith, it seems, could remove mountains, has in a book which treats of faces, asserted that the nose is no cheat and that he can see every man's character sitting astride on his nose.

This is a whimsical age. Who would believe that a man could be found sufficiently bold, and readers sufficiently credulous, to suppose that Favor is not deceitful.

More than forty years since, when my grandmother suffered my elder brother to lead me by the hand into company, I was pleased with all faces. "You, charming maid," says I to a smiling lass, "have a benevolent countenance; You must lend a favourable ear to my vows." A sudden coquettish wave of her fan and a scorning nose proved that *Favor was deceitful*.

A buyer goes into a country store and, leaning over the counter, asks the shopkeeper for changeable silk. He holds up a piece in a favorable point of view, and smiling plausibly, declaims an hour upon its cheapness and durability. The silk is bought; when daughter Dolly had worn it two Sundays it was still changeable; spotted with bilge water and torn by a pin, even one eye might read on the hem that *Favour is deceitful*.

I recollect that, during my nonage, I rested many hopes upon the plausibility of a simpering courtier. He had been educated by the Jesuits, noted for giant promise and pigmy performance. This man had a sweet smile and a silver tongue. His smile and tongue were worth a prince's ransom to him. He had a wonderful knack of being agreeable; as to being useful, that was of no consequence. He set up a school for smiling and his pupils might there learn to nod and smirk cash away from the purse. Nothing obstructed this man; every road was a river road to him; his neighbors called him the smoothing plane; he removed all asperities. But all was "false and hollow." He planed away the rough planks of life, it is true, but he kept the shavings himself. The man was selfish, and his *Favor was deceitful*.

I saw lately a morose wretch with a book in his hand. His urchin form reminded me of a gnarly crab apple, at once misshapen and sour; the leaves he turned over were Sterne's, and his cheeks were moistened by the death of Lefevre. How, whispered I, can this man boast sensibility? I know him well,—a grinder of poverty's face, who understands distress and sale better than a deputy sheriff; this is he who drives away the cottager's cow, and plucks from under her the widow's bed. I paused, and reflexion convinced me that his was a mechanical and crocodile grief, that though he wept, he could wound, and that his *Favor was deceitful*.

Thomas Paine, that infidel in religion and that visionary in politics, seduces many of you, my countrymen. You read his *Age of Reason*, and think the Bible a last year's almanac; you read his *Rights of Man* and think government slavery, and Washington an imposter. But the man who labors to destroy the pious hope, or to raise the ferment of faction, is an enemy to your peace. Be your devotions and your government equally undisturbed; attendance at church at least preserves your neatness and sociability. Obedience to government causes you to sit in peace under the fig tree. Trust me, he who jeers received truths, or who tells you that there is no distinction among men and that *all* are equally qualified to govern, is an imposter more pernicious than Mahomet, and his *Favor is deceitful*.

VI

"And he will be a wild man."

IF a young fellow, at every tavern frolic, insists upon paying the piper; if you see many hundred yards of tobacco and gaudy vest-patterns charged, and long tails of dittos drawn out on the trader's book, believe the Lay Preacher that such a hair-brained, extravagant youth is on the high road towards a certain public edifice noted for its strength, "and he will be a wild man."

Many an honest American farmer and his wife, who formerly were in constant terror of Indians and shut themselves in garrisons and forts to avoid captivity, suppose that, now these wild men of the woods are exterminated by rum, there is room for fear no longer. But there are wild men roaming about yet, even in towns which lie many a league from Indian settlements. The wild men whom I now describe, it is true, have neither feathers on their heads nor moggisons on their feet; jewels are not pendent from their noses nor blankets thrown round their limbs, but still they are dangerous and wild creatures as much as if they traversed the woods of Huron, navigated Lake Mumphramagog, or hunted in the Tenesee.

When you hear six pair of sleigh bells jingling along the road about two o'clock in a winter morning, when you hear many a drunken curse from the driver, and learn from a tavern keeper that the owner of the aforesaid sleigh and bells paid twenty shillings club of the reckoning, he is a wild man broke loose from his keeper, and will hardly be tamed.

The prediction contained in my text was applied to Ishmael, and has been remarkably verified in his descendants, the Arabs. But this roving and lawless people the generality of geographers and Christians suppose confined to the extended plains of Asia, and dream not that any of the tribe inhabit this continent. But Ishmaelites, wild as their ancestors, abound; and in the shape of horse jockeys, high bucks, and hard drinkers, manifest their wildness a thousand ways.

[14]

THE LAY PREACHER

The mention of horse jockeys "moves me from my natural moderation." As the jockey is a very common and fashionable character, too, in most villages, his celebrity deserves some consideration. The Lay Preacher acknowledges that he, like most sedentary parsons, is an awkward rider, and sits too much in his easy chair to sit gracefully on a horse. Still, as he is pleased with beauty and grace wherever found, he cannot but be struck with the figure of a noble animal distinguished for those enchanting qualities. He warmly approves, therefore, those who exercise humanity towards the generous steed, and who to an animal which safely bears them a rugged journey are liberal of hay and sparing of the lash. He even allows to men of property the indulgence of taste and whim in choosing a creature of so much elegance and use. But when a man so far forgets his dignity as to prefer the stable to the parlour, to be the constant companion of ostlers, to use no language but that of the turf, and wear life away in combing a mane, one cannot avoid thinking that the beast he curries is the nobler animal. A more serious objection can be made to the professed jockey. He not only devotes too much time to the stable but exercises too much craft in the purchase and sale of his favorite animal. He not only, like Richard in the play, cries, "A horse, a horse, a kingdom for a horse," but deems it not only pardonable but praiseworthy to get what is called the advantage. This phrase means to sell an article for treble its worth, and to make the bargain by falsehood and by fraud! The jockey and the gamester have been frequently compared, but he who sports with cards, rarely cheats, except when his adversary is a sharper. Even the gamester has too much honor to cajole the weak and unskilful. But the jockey professes to be a rogue, and even glories in defrauding, so that he and his associates might with propriety hang out a board inscribed, in the phrase of M'Fingal, "Beelzebub and Co." Of all the wild characters that infest a country town, a low and knavish jockey is the most depraved; his hand, like that of Ishmael, "is against every man." That it may prove nerveless, but that on the contrary "every man's hand" may be successful against him, must be the wish of every honest man in the community, and is the prayer of the Lay Preacher.

[15]

VII

"By this craft we have our wealth."

DEMETRIUS, the silversmith, and "others of the like occupation," of whom such honourable mention is made in the Acts of the Apostles, are not the only persons who, after playing, like sharpers, the game of interest, can turn around and cry, "Ye know, Sirs, that by this *craft* we have our wealth."

All the world resorted to church when Parson Plagiary preached. The old women snivelled, and the deacons groaned in unison with the "vocal nose" of the parson. The bucks went to hear him, for he was short, and did not kindle hellfire in his pulpit. The ladies praised his white hand and vowed that he adjusted the cushion gracefully. The Parson's reputation and salary increased. Sometimes a reformed rake would send him a cask of wine, to animate his divinity, and sometimes the ladies would go a shopping to "Vanity Fair" with Madam and purchase her a dressy cap. Thus our Parson, enjoying more than a disciple's share of the "loaves and fishes," together with a stock of wine from abroad—and of oil at home, went on from one degree of ease to another, ate full dinners, drank wine literally for his stomach's sake, and then, with a book in his hand, went into his study to—sleep. He grew lazy, copied pages from Dr. Blair, sometimes stole a whole sermon from Sterne, and by this *craft*, not only had wealth but fame. Verily, brothers of the pulpit, this was profitable priestcraft!

But of all crafts, a quack doctor's craft is the most crafty. It is one of the easiest trades in life. It is not, like Jacob's apprenticeship, a seven years' labour, but like some chapman's books that I used to read when a boy, is "familiar to the meanest capacity." The receipt to make a quack is shorter than the shortest in his Dispensatory: Take the first blockhead you can find, get credit for him at the apothecary's for a pound of cortex, mount him on a pied horse, and bid him speak guttural words. Depend on it that my friend the German surgeon, who has been regularly bred at a

THE LAY PREACHER

foreign university and who detects by a glance the morbid and peccant cause, will be neglected; his lancets will rust in shagreen while the triumphant pretender has full license to kill, to enter houses, leading captive "silly women," and by this craft to have his wealth.

The country attorney—I do not mean him who eloquently defends and generously charges his clients, but that pettifogging scrivener, synonymous all over the world with scoundrel—the country attorney who inflames village disputes, who sues for nine pence, who buys notes of hand cheap and sells them dear, who after receiving ten thousand pounds as his "wages of iniquity," still runs about haunting Justices' doors, inquiring "who will show him any good," who will serve a precept upon the poor widow and compel her to cast in her last mite into his treasury, is a near relation to Demetrius and all the silversmith family, and by this cursed craft has his wealth.

Some of the Lay Preacher's friends reproach him for his labours in an age when few read, fewer remember, and none believe sermons. Some advise him to sell all he has, and with the merchant in the gospel, to seek "goodly pearls." Others propose a journey to New York, and talk with rapture of the schemes of a speculator. This advice has the usual fate; it only serves to confirm prior resolutions. Preferring literary to land speculations, and happy to amuse the vacant and inform the simple, he studies with zeal to imitate Dr. Franklin and "The Prompter," and, indolent at his parsonage, thinks some, and smokes the tranquil cigar more. From this humble "craft" is derived the "wealth" of the Lay Preacher.

VIII

"In those days there was no king in Israel; every man did what was right in his own eyes."

AND when there is no energetic government in America, each of her subjects will do so too. Do not be offended, my readers, because, this week, I choose to delineate *political* rather than *moral* truth. You know that, from the establishment of papacy to the time of Archbishop Laud, the Church has always affected an anxiety for the State. I should not be a true Preacher were I not sometimes to forget that our order are ministers of the Prince of Peace. The enforcement of virtue and the reproof of the sinner do not always delight. We must sometimes speculate on the decree of Caesar, that all the world should be taxed, and sometimes inquire whence come wars and fightings among men. As the Whig divines in 1775 were instrumental in destroying the old government, perhaps a Federal parson may offer some reasons against subverting the new.

The studies of theology and the labour of writing these sermons do not occupy the whole of each week. I have leisure to talk politics with my neighbors and to read many of the newspapers from the southward. From them, and occasionally from an evening's chat with some traveller from Boston, I learn that certain restless and perturbed spirits, under the plausible title of "Democrats," are labouring anxiously to teach proselytes the soothing doctrines of liberty and equality. Liberty such as the fish-women of Paris enjoyed when they treated a Queen of France like a prostitute of the stews; and Equality such as a Legendre and Santerre could boast when the butcher's stall of the one, and brewer's dray of the other, were, in a Revolutionary government, on a level with the throne. I have been in the habit for many years, my readers, of turning over authors who wrote in the earliest ages of the world, men who understood the meaning of the word "Liberty" as well at least as the moderns. From these books—and they are of the highest authority—I have learned that civil liberty consists in doing whatever does not militate with laws, restraining individual excesses to promote the public weal. Observation has further suggested that there are a few, and how few! upon whom the Parent of wisdom has largely bestowed that ethereal spirit, that bold and sublime genius which He has chosen to withhold from the majority of mankind. Yet farther, it is obvious that in the race for riches, all run, and still but few reach the goal and bear the prize. It follows, therefore, that he of ample mind or ample purse will direct the councils and command the service of him who is weak or poor, and that equality is a visionary whim. God and nature having created such eternal distinctions, how presumptuous, how unavailing for an American bankrupt to proclaim in the market place to his deluded hearers that they had been amused with an old wives' fable, but that the servant might roam where he list, like his master, and that the plough boy, conscious of equality, might journey to Philadelphia and claim the Presidency from Washington.

I am persuaded that St. Paul possessed as erect and independent a spirit, and as much sincerity, as any leader of a club throughout the Union. The government of his own country was a vice royalty, and probably, therefore, a capricious and arbitrary one. He had visited Rome, felt the power of its emperors, and lived for years in subjection to laws which we usually term despotic. Yet this amiable apostle and man of the world, though bold and original in plan and execution, was so convinced of the utility of order and due subordination that, in his epistle to the Romans, who, under the reign of Nero, would have been gratified by revolutionary logic, he charges every soul to be subject unto the higher powers. It is worthy of remark, and will show how important the subject was considered by the apostle, that he maintains the proposition not by political but religious arguments, for after declaring that all power was derived from above, he concludes regularly that resistance to "ordained" government was opposition to the supreme will.

I have examined very carefully this great man's epistles to various cities of the East, a quarter of the globe coerced by the sternest laws, and cannot find a single sentence to induce change of officers or a popular government. Neither Corinthians nor Ephesians are advised to club subordination away. The funding system of Rome is tactily approved, for Paul enjoins a rigorous payment of the public debt, and if an ambassador were sent to negotiate a treaty with the faithless Parthians or the hostile Medes, the Saint did not, when the envoy returned, call upon his god to curse him, or curse him himself.

But suppose, my countrymen, that we should consider it superfluous to have a King, or what is the same, good government, in Israel, and that every man should be permitted to do what was right in his own eyes. Why, at the great public table, if each were allowed to carve for himself, what tid bits would the great scramblers devour, and what a sorry meal would the majority make! I am convinced that if the fantastic vision of "Equality" could be realized, and men were to roam at large in the wilds of freedom, that many would faint by the way and that more would hanker after those savory herbs of Egypt they had abjured. We should be guilty of every species of outrage and excess. We should hear the voice of wild misrule, in darkness, and the mob that rageth, at noon day. If there was no king in Israel, not to mention what the women would play, men would play the rogue with impunity, and neither life nor property would be secure. That experiment in politics we are now trying in America, if democratic projectors persevere in interrupting the process, would fail ridiculously, and tyrants might then aver that mankind, instead of being free by nature, were doomed to be slaves.

X

"Little children, keep yourselves from idols."

THIS precept of the Evangelist was not intended for the nursery. Infants of the largest growth, we know, have their rattles and "idols," and the "little children" whom John meant to keep safe were men and women who had reached the full measure of their stature but who, from levity, might prove too attached to objects "earthly" or "devilish."

A learned commentator upon this passage might here exclaim, "O blind Lay Preacher, worthy to be classed with the foolish Galatians, cannot you perceive that your text was designed merely as a warning against the worship of images set up by the superstition of pagans, and that the Gentiles were the little children?" This is too partial and narrow an explanation. I am willing to suppose that John, like other zealous Christians of that age, was anxious to strip each Roman temple of its false god. But the Evangelist well knew that there were idols, the objects of fond adoration, besides brazen or ivory statues of Jupiter and Mercury. In this enlightened period, when altars are no more and the smoke of heathen sacrifice no longer ascends, numerous idols are reverenced; and when the Lay Preacher enumerates their names all his readers will agree with him that those who bow the knee to these modern Baals are "little children," always weak and sometimes wicked.

A number of pretty women of my acquaintance, have and will, in spite of my lessons, set up a certain smooth-faced idol on the top of their toilets. They call it a looking glass, and worship it hourly. This is a most pernicious idol, a great cheat of their time and an artful flatterer of their beauty. They straightway retire and forget what manner of persons they should prove. They forget the fond husband and are deaf to the pathetic wailings of the child. They become impatient of every domestic duty, and are careful alone, with much care, to be decked in purple and perfumed with all powders of the merchant. Little Misses, listen to a friend; break your idol—it is brittle, I assure you—read instructive books and sometimes, on a Sunday, sermons—much better ones, I mean, than those of the Lay Preacher.

Another species of glass is a more fashionable idol than the one recently described. Its name, ye topers haunting the temple of excess, is drinking glass. In devotion to this bewitching idol I have seen whole companies so absorbed with elevated eyes and outstretched hands, that until I heard execration I could almost fancy them penitent and pious. Reeling, hic-cupping, and lisping, what nearer resemblance to "little children" who stammer and sprawl can be discovered than those sottish worshippers of wine, who have all the imbecility of infancy, without its innocence.

The sons of Sloth might be supposed so sunken in sleep as to be incapable of that degree of activity necessary for prostration to an idol. But the ingenuity of the sluggard's mind seems to supply, in this instance, the want of bodily exertion. Like those torpid monks who have contrived, not to court piety abroad but, to preclude long journeys, keep her semblance in their cell, the sluggard, if I may so express it, has domesticated his idol. He does not even wake to bow himself before it, but, supine in bed, fondly hugs his pillow! Could snorers be roused from this dream and put away this strange god, how, in the beautiful phrase of Dr. Young, "would it bless mankind, and rescue me."

Popularity is a great idol, sought with more assiduity than ever Dagon was by the Philistines. What sacrifices are daily offered it by the seekers of office and by the demagogues of faction. To the discontented, the desperate, the debtor, and the designing, at Boston and Philadelphia, might not a sober man, whether cloathed with the divine authority of the author of my text or with the crow-coloured coat of the Lay Preacher, exclaim, "Ye *little* patriots, keep yourselves from this idol! With what wild vagaries does it agitate your plotting heads and your beating hearts. How your pretended love of your country causes you to forget Washington, guardian and soldier, your first love! How it causes care to sit on your faded cheeks! How it detains you ingloriously in the dirty lanes and 'Green Dragons' of sedition, scribbling saucy toasts and vamping rash resolves against the treaties and laws of your land, which, smiling in peace, seems to scorn your impotency. Forsake, therefore, those French fashions which sit so awkwardly upon the sedate American. Be no longer the irregular sectaries of revolt, but join the venerable and established Church of government."

[22]

XI

"Drink waters out of thine own cistern, and running waters out of thine own well."

SUCH waters will be more exhilarating to an independent spirit than wine at another man's board.

In our free and independent government, the habits of its citizens should partake of its character. Happily for the dignity and well-being of the Americans, that most useful and most numerous class, the landed interest, are signalized for deriving their wealth from their own fields and slaking their thirst at the peculiar spring. Even the jealousy of England has acknowledged the unpalatable truth, and Guthrie, a Scottish and servile geographer, has recorded the American farmer's freedom. What order of knighthood can be more noble than yeomen, laborious and rich? Who has a better title of dominion than he who is prince of his own pasture and feeds his fattening flocks, rejoicing under his shepherd sway? The peasants of Poland and the Turkish slaves of a sultan or vizier may acquire, but they cannot *preserve*. To them independence is a phantom at which they grasp, and find nothing but chains. Here each man may be the artificer of his own fortune, and when the goodly fabric is erected, no griping landlord is heard to demand a rent.

To such an exalted point, more sublime than the throne of a prince, it is the binding duty of aspiring and manly youth to arise. Independence is an eagle's wing which exalts to those elevations whence we can have a bird's-eye view of all that men covet, the brilliant and the bold. But when the meanness of dependence degrades us among Lazarus and the dogs, to subsist on the falling crumbs from a superior's table, we are little removed from the servile spaniel, and like him might be collared and fetch and carry for a master.

He who in earnest seeks after independence, shall, like Solomon's inquirer after wisdom, have no great travel, for he shall find her sitting at his doors. Nor will she be coy to enter them but will inhabit there if honesty and industry are of that house.

[23]

THE LAY PREACHER

Let the pilgrim through this world disdain to subsist on alms, but refresh himself from his *own* scrip, and instead of accepting from a great woman at Shunem, or any other lady of quality, a bed, a table, a stool, or a candlestick, let him rather build, with his own scantlings, a chamber in the wall and furnish it himself.

Hearken, ye ardent and erect spirits who, full of expectation, enter on the stage of action, hearken to the warning voice of Prudence and the Preacher. Be *independent* in your property. Lean not against another man, lest you continue not long in one stay. Trust only yourselves, and be not over much trusted by the merchant. When you think you can afford two coats, purchase but one. Put a small piece of silver into your purse each day and you will feel proud to find it swollen at the year's end. Be more willing to lend than to borrow, and be careful, if the borrower call, to have something to lend. Observing these easy rules you will sleep quietly, undisturbed by the dun; when you go singing by the wayside, not a tailor will present his bill, nor a sheriff pluck you by the sleeve.

XII

"Remove sorrow far from thee: for sorrow hath killed many, and there is no profit therein."

DRY up your eyes then, ye mourners; for grief will not restore the friends you have lost nor abate the edge of misfortune, but as oil and the whetstone to the razor, it will sharpen that which is already too acute, and the bleeding heart will show a still deeper wound. Why will you strive to add one drop to this "vale of tears" which, trust me, is already too full; why court the acquaintance of Grief, that sorry companion who, sobbing and silent as he journeys with you through the wilderness of this world, multiplies every brake, and adds tenfold horror to the gloom? You have various and real ills to encounter in your sore travail; the climate is vaporous, and you must be sick; men are treacherous, and you will be deceived. Poverty will sometimes start up "like an armed man" before you, and your careful days be those of an hireling. But be of good cheer; and repeat not in the day of adversity, with erring Solomon, that laughter is mad, nor impertinently inquire of Mirth what doeth she, but believe with my predecessor, Sterne, that comfortable assertion worth a million of cold homilies, that every time we smile, and still more every time we laugh, it adds something to the fragment of life.

No profit therein! No verily; the man of sorrow who, with sullen Ahab, refuses to eat bread and changes his time for tears, is engaged in one of the most barren and least lucrative employments you can conceive. Sighs I have always considered as the very canker of the heart, and sobs the grand epitomizers of existence. Child of melancholy! if sorrow hath killed many, and there is no profit therein, banish it from thy shades; for why, in the pathetic language of Ecclesiastes, shouldst thou die before thy time?

But who are those fair forms, the one with folded arms and the other with bounding step, ministering, O kindly handmaids, at the bedside of the Philosopher? I see his pallid cheek already flush; I hear his voice utter a bolder tone; wrinkles are no more seen on his brow, and not a solitary tear traces a lonely way down his cheek; for Patience and Mirth are before him. At their salutary approach, the troop of cares, the family of pain, fly disconsolate and free the vacant heart from their torturing sway. Gentle and benignant spirits, meekest Patience and chirping Mirth, whether my cottage be unroofed by the storm or my couch thorned by disease, whether friends grow lukewarm or lovers be put far away, let your gay forms appear, and the load of life will no more be irksome: For well I know your pleasing arts. I well remember your numerous topics of consolation: your music, your song, your carelessness, Mirth and Patience, your philosophy and resignation. Sorrow, as the wise son of Sirach tells us, may kill many, but ye can make alive. Come, then, to the unfortunate, and let the adverse hour be your favorite hour of visitation.

XIII

"What aileth thee?"

TO what countless sick people might this question be proposed, and yet not one of the number be really ill, in the medical sense of the word. But there exists in some individuals an ill habit of mind, a sickness of the heart, a lameness of spirit, diseases more difficult to cure than cancer, fever, or gout. A good-natured patient, swallowing his physicians's prescription, may become free of a sick room and walk at large with health's reddest roses blooming on his cheek. But a man of morbid anxiety, fretfulness, ambition, or avarice will send in vain for the healing drug of the apothecary. His wounds are of so rancorous, festering, incurable nature, they will demand much time to heal and many medicines to assuage. Though the whole medical society should consult, though Turkey should yield all her poppies and the balm of Gilead trickle from a thousand jars, the cancer of the heart mocks the healing power; and often the fell malady is commensurate with life.

In morning and devious rambles through lonely pasture or gloomy wood, far from the clink of Industry's anvil, far from the jocund chorus of Music's songs, I meet a meagre and moping hypocondriac. His temples do not throb, but they are bound, not with the chaplets of spring but with a white handkerchief, the flag of headache and disease. The day is genial, for it is one of the mildest in May, but doubled and trebled stockings on his legs, thick waistcoats closely buttoned over the breast, and a ponderous greatcoat enveloping the man, attest the nature and magnitude of his fears. He shivers at a blast impregnated with flowers, and when all nature is warm he dreads taking cold. What a disease, and what stubborn symptoms, which acknowledge no cause! I have a right to say "no cause," for well I know the fate and fortune of this splenetic. The first is happy, and the other ample. Blest with birth, with talents, with family, with favor, have not I a privilege to inquire of him with more than common curiosity, "What aileth thee? Why is thy brilliant spirit cast down, and why is thy generous soul troubled?"

What aileth thee, O lawyer, that after having drawn ten thousand pounds from the purses of thy cajoled clients, thou still must play thy saving and cheating game? In thy old age, when thou seest in thy coffers the rewards of thy dark and spider-like industry, canst thou still be unsatisfied and wish to make more writs against innocent defendants? What is thy object? Is it wealth? You have a fortune. Is it reputation? What fame is it to bellow in support of thy declarations, which will soon be forgotten with the causes they supported? Believe me, you had better write one page of history, couple two feeble lines of rhyme, or utter one moment's melodious breath than to defend right and wrong as you do, without discrimination. For shame; is it not enough to have the silly vanity of tickling rural jurors' ears in your youth, but you must confound them in your middle age, and persevere in duping them in the decline of life? Hasten and make amends; the night of repentance is coming on, and it will be a night of thick and Egyptian darkness to thee!

XIV

"Come, my beloved, let us go forth into the field; let us lodge in the villages."

THE hope of gain and the love of society have now, for centuries, incited men to risk many inconveniences for the sake of congregating in cities. The simple would naturally conclude that where there was "much people" there would be much jollity. Desperate adventurers bringing their craft to market would have nothing to lose and everything to gain in the throng. Ambition would find in every street a ladder lofty enough to reach the extent of many a project; and Avarice could find no place more convenient to drive a bargain than a frequented coffee house or an obscure alley. Schemes of wealth and aggrandizement or pleasure thus operating upon hope, the busiest and most sanguine passion, should we wonder to mark flocks of rovers, eager and upon the wing, expecting by a flight from the country to fly from themselves?

But wisely has the wise man said, "Better is a handful with quietness than both hands full, with travail and vexation of spirit." Tranquility chooses the country for her favorite residence, and should you inquire for the peaceable personage in town, every cit would tell you he did not know her and that she must be some outlandish person. In cities I grant there are many agitations, which are dignified by the name of pleasure, but they are a spurious brood, and felicity would not call them her own. The streams of pleasure in cities are like their common sewers; they are turbid, they are full of taint. He who quaffs liberally must soon be either sick or drunk; and such morbid influence have they on the brain that men go from them, like the apostle's gazer in the glass, "not knowing what manner of person they were."

They who wish never to be cloyed, to respire with freedom, to enjoy the pleasure of reading and reflection, and to sleep sweetly must go forth into the field, and lodge in villages. Allowing that there are some genuine delights in the thronged town, yet they tread too fast on each other and weary by constant succession. A man will pray sometimes no less fervently for a respite from pleasure, than in a fit of the gout for a respite from pain. The pleasures of the country, pure, simple, not dazzling, not boistrous, will gently stir the stream of life—a stream which passion should not be suffered to vex into whirlpool nor be "creamed over and mantled" by the stagnation of sloth. To saunter along the banks of the brook and allure the trout from his recess, to crop the fantastic flowers of May or the strawberries of June, to climb the solemn mountain or loiter in the valley's shade are cheap and real pleasures, make no man a criminal, and leave no sting behind.

Such is the influence of the atmosphere upon the human body that even robust constitutions are sensible of the changes of the air, and invalids are "tremblingly alive" to them. A fluid that, whether we are sheltered at home or exposed abroad, we are obliged perpetually to dabble in, we should attempt to find in the utmost purity. But in great towns, on the margin of the main, reeking with the putrefaction of its shores; in cities whose streets are defiled with frequent feet and scorched by the dog-star, where every tenth house is a hospital, it is not air which the sallow inhabitants breathe, but "a mass of offensive things." Let the chain which binds willing prisoners to the crowd be broken, let them "go forth to the field," and if the easy play of their lungs and alertness of limbs, if the light slumber and the red cheek will not convince them whence the mighty change in their health has proceeded, they deserve to die soon, and in some dirty lane, as a punishment for their incredulity.

Dissipation being the characteristic of cities, to travel its round will require so much time that none will be left to cultivate the understanding or mend the heart. Whatever some indolent fine ladies and fine gentlemen may suppose, we were not sent into this world merely to go to assemblies, to saunter at shops, to purchase of milliners, or undergo the three hours' operation of a barber. He who wishes to read verses or write them, he who means to instruct others or commune with himself, must seek the retirement of the "field" and the "village." In the city, protracted dinners and midnight revel will murder half and more than the day, and the long repose of the morning will be necessary to repair the wasted spirit. In solitude, as there are few incidents to enchain the mind and few excesses to debase it, the student will bring a willing intellect to the complicated task, and from a pen put to a rural desk all difficulty and hindrance will vanish away. He who in city and broken slumbers has a thousand times turned his pillow and himself and, like Shakespeare's king, has muttered, "O partial sleep, how have I frighted thee?" will find that if he would sleep soundly he must "lodge in the village." That exercise which in the country is usually taken in the day will induce that lassitude ever accompanied by delicious repose at night. He may be assured that at the close of the day the hamlet is still; no lumbering carts or chariots will banish his pleasant dreams, no outcry of midnight murder chill his palpitating heart. No noise will strike his ear but the distant waterfall, and no fires glitter in his eye but the innoxious one of the lucid insect of the meadows. At this genial period, when every June rose is broad blown and the garniture of the fields is of the greenest hue, the emigrant from town may, perhaps, find some amusement not inferior to gambling all night, tracing dusty streets, or visiting the sagacious dog. He will acknowledge the flavour of our strawberry equal to his pineapple, and the notes of the robin and wren "of little quill" may soothe him as much, and sound as sweet, as those of the songstress of the theater.

XV

"My head, My head."

THIS is an exclamation which authors may make with as much propriety as the son of the Shunammite.

Bitter complaints have been uttered by saints of yore against that lawless member, the tongue. But it has fared with the engine of speech as with any other mere tool; it has frequently suffered for the faults of its principles. The tongue is an active agent, but quite harmless, unless set in motion or instigated to evil by the head.

When Job had been maltreated by some Jacobin, of Uz perhaps, who wished for a revolution in favour of some insinuating democrat, the wish of Job, "O that my enemy had written a book," though apparently enigmatical, is one of the most pertinent and least absurd wishes recorded in history.

Profound knowledge of the world taught him not to pray that his foe, by some sudden impulse or some sanguinary passion, might render himself obnoxious to justice. He knew that in mercy's code there was perpetually a saving clause in favour of the errors of the heart, but that for the deliberate effusions of the head there was no proviso. He knew that to pronounce his enemy a knave, though it might put the wary Jews on their guard when he proffered a pledge or proposed a bargain, would among an usurious tribe noted for the spirit of trade, render him an object of respect rather than of contempt. The irritated man of Uz, therefore, with singular sagacity, implores that he might write a book. The vanity of authorship, Job probably argued, will induce him to publish ideas crude or absurd, and criticizing Uzzites will then ridicule the fool. His neglected volume not even the "wayfaring men" shall peruse, and its leaves shall curl the hair or cool the "crisping pins" of the oriental maidens.

From the above history of what probably passed in Job's mind it will appear that it was his decided opinion nothing could be so injurious to his enemy as a bad head, if its owner should hazard a public exposure of its thoughts. So few heads are capable of framing useful books that the chance was that a foolish one would

[32]

be produced by that author who, in opposition to all the East, was presumptuous and depraved enough to be the avowed enemy of a popular citizen. Such an arrogant scribbler would either commit himself by dogmatical assertion, or alarm others by libertine argument; his book would be too trite for the wise, or too obscure for the simple.

Thomas Paine, could he survey that numerous herd transformed from credulous Christians to infidels by his *Age of Reason*, and from good subjects to revolters by his *Common Sense*, would sigh for the mischief he had wrought, and even at the ninth hour, before he was drunken, would exclaim, "My head, my head!"

Were not the subject almost too serious to allow the sportive style, we might indulge, and hint that some of the legislators of France, sensible of the many evils of heads, invented a summary mode of lopping those excrescencies. King, noble, and priest have been visited by a malady similar to that which vexed the Shunammite's son; and each has ascended a sanguinary scaffold, ejaculating "My head, my head!"

Daring and impudent as it may appear in this levelling age to avow respect for birth or talents, I confess, as a little of the aristocratical leaven has possibly leavened the whole lump, that my notions on this subject are very old-fashioned. My own head is so weak that I cannot help fancying some difference in the capacity of those of other men. I shall not, therefore, say a word to the prejudice of the ancient and honourable families of Longheads or Wiseheads, but shall wish them a quiet repose on their ancient foundations, and that neither a Frenchman nor a Virginian should abridge their immunities nor disturb their possession. For the head of genius whose ancestry can be traced beyond William the Conqueror, and whose talents are so confessedly brilliant, I feel peculiarly solicitous. I at first thought of wishing it a place in the museum of Cambridge, but am apprehensive lest it should sustain a rude kick from some of the animals of the place or have its fine features marred by the fogginess of the atmosphere. I therefore consign it to the charge of Philenia, and already behold it crowned with chaplets of immortal verdure.

XVI

"Go thy way, eat thy bread with joy, and drink thy wine with a merry heart."

AND where is the sullen mortal who would refuse to obey so pleasant an injunction as this, coming, too, on the authority of Solomon?

However, as this doctrine at first view seems to flatter the indulgence of the passions, and therefore to proceed with an ill grace from a moral teacher, let us look narrowly into Solomon's system and endeavor that Wisdom may be justified of her children.

In one of the most interesting and amusing journals that we find in the Bible, Solomon has narrated to us the hopes and fears which agitated his busy life. Born a monarch, he could exercise supreme power; and a courtier of the muses, he acquired the highest wisdom. His city was magnificent, his subjects loyal. Commerce wafted him all that was rare from Sidon, and the decks of Tarshish ships glittered with the pageantry of its peacocks. In a situation so favorable to enjoyment, it was natural that he should withold his heart from no joy and that the luxury of the East should excite him to refine on pleasure. From his love of letters, his first indulgences were of course mental. He conned the pithy sayings of Orientals and fatigued his faculties with the scholastic jargon of many a Rabbi. But soon discovering that he was directing his thoughts through a trackless maze, and that if such abstruse disquisitions were too eargerly pursued, Wisdom would turn into Folly and too much learning make him mad, he resolved to descend from the pinnacle of speculation, and mix with men in the highway of life. We then hear of his agricultural experiments, the cares of a numerous household, his domestic details, and his public munificence. Through the dusty deserts of Palestine he probably conveyed distant water to thirsty subjects, and with numerous bridges over-arched the brook Cedron. But the restless Prince, when the labors of the day were past and he communed with his own heart in the inner chamber of the palace, found, in reflection's sober hour, that this was a sore travail and vexation of spirit. At length, after numerous experiments on happiness, he drew a formal comparison between the various situations in life. After stating the accompt of human hope and disappointment, with clerical accuracy: that Folly has a funeral splendid as the obsequies of Wisdom herself; that the goods of fortune are perishable and, though attained by a course of painful industry, may probably become the inheritance of an idler; that the reign of novelty was past and every object wore the uniform of sameness, he concludes, I think philosophically, by arguing against anxiety and enjoining a moderate participation of festal joys.

From various passages interspersed throughout the volume of our belief I am persuaded that Christianity was designed to be a cheerful system. Miserable was the perversion of its precepts by those in early times who believed that none could prove its sincere votaries but the moping and the austere. It is wonderful that primitive Piety, who must be supposed to hold the Bible constantly in her hand, should not discern the numerous texts enjoined to sanctify the moderate use of the good things of this world. Not to be too anxious, to hope habitually, to enjoy soberly, and to rejoice evermore are prominent precepts in the New Testament. I hope I shall not be accused of thinking like certain philosophers of the sect of the Epicureans, when I frankly acknowledge that I see no valid reason to forbid the straitest of our religion eating a dinner with sweet herbs instead of the bitter ones of the Passover. Should such a feast of joy provoke thrist, I shall not deem it an infraction of gospel rules to indulge him with a little wine. The vineyards of Engedi are no more, but those of France remain; and if a Jewish lawgiver could "tie his colt to the vine, and dip his mantle in the blood of the grape," why may not the sober glass be tinged, and why were grapes given us, unless to be crushed?

XVII

"Hate not laborious work, neither husbandry."

THE snow beginning now* to trickle fast from the hills, and spots of green sward to appear, the provident husbandman, refreshed by the rest of winter, thinks it time to leave the afternoon mug of cider unfinished and prepare for the labours of spring. But as many, attached to ease and the fireside, are unwilling to put their hands to the plough, and wishing, in the common phrase of our country, that six weeks' sledding in March may put off the evil day of furrowing the fields, I will endeavour to convince them that nothing is so laborious as having nothing to do.

If a fretful farmer who in some rainy day thinks no employment is so toilsome as that which he exercises, will cast his eyes upon the various idlers sauntering along with pale cheeks and gouty limbs, from Dan to Beersheba, he will be convinced that mowing in July and haling wood in winter are less fatiguing than pleasure's race. When an inquisitive being asks why there is so much vice and misery in this world, I conceive no answer would be more pertinent than because the vicious and miserable have, at some period of their lives, been haters of laborious work and husbandry.

What is it but this aversion to labor, and a fantastic wish to be free from care, that urges so many to exchange wheat for whisky and their money for a game of cards? Why do such numbers beg at rich men's doors? Why are so many rheumatic limbs propped by crutches and staves? Why does the attorney commence such frequent suits for the innkeeper? And why are the debtor's rooms in a jail crowded? If the hoe, the spade, and the field could speak, they would say, because men hearken to the whispers of fancy and forsake us, their best allies in life's warfare.

Unless the sower goeth forth to sow, he cannot expect sixty or an hundred fold. Unless men sometimes love laborious work and

---

*In March.

husbandry, they will not reckon much fine gold nor be eagerly inquired after in the gate. The ages of miracles are past, and I know not whether man has a right to expect that Providence will interpose particularly in his favor and give him bread, if he will not be at the pains to leaven it.

That ancient adjudication which sentenced Adam to eat bread in the sweat of his brow has been harshly denominated a curse by unthinking Christians. But it is demonstrable that the necessity for labor is one of the highest blessings of life, and without this necessity other blessings would lose half their value. The ancient poets, delighting in fiction, have amused themselves and credulous readers with a gorgeous description of the golden age— an age, which according to poetical chronology, existed prior to the primal curse. In this blest period, no coulter pierced earth's surface, honey distilled from oaks, and wine and milk gurgled spontaneously from springs. This is undoubtedly a vision of the night. But if it had been realized, and men, like the austere governor in the gospel, could have reaped where they had not sown and gathered where they had not strewed, such a state of inaction would produce an extreme of weariness more intolerable than the drudgery of the field. A profound observer has remarked that if all the year were playing holidays, to sport would be as tedious as to work; and if we mark the men of pleasure whom the legacy or the partiality of parents has enriched, we shall discover the truth of the observation. Who is so anxious, who loses so much rest, who so worketh with his hands, as the nocturnal gamester? What perils, what storms, what fatigue the drunkard encounters, navigating the raging ocean of wine; yet it is these who make delight a trade and what should be the occasional relaxation, the business of life. For myself, I cannot help thinking that cutting tender grass is more easy than cutting unlucky cards; that the laborer with a corn basket on his shoulder is less burdened than the tipler with the load of his stomach; and that the flaxen-head ploughboy, tracing the straight and undeviating furrow, has a lighter task to fulfil than he who bewilders himself in the mazes of wantonness and seeks those daughters of Zion who walk with stretched-forth necks.

Go, then, happy husbandmen, with alacrity to laborious work. Trust me, ye sleep sounder than him who advises you and who is destined to have no acres to till, but who, with throbbing temples, toils over the weekly sermon. I gaze with pleasure at your bursting barns, your well-ordered cottages, and your fruitful fields. I see that in consequence of your labor you are healthful and happy. While your valuable exertions continue, your country will never grieve. Continue to venerate the plough and to feed the ox, and you will turn up gold with the one, and draw to your dwellings most fine gold with the other.

XVIII

"There is a lion in the streets."

TRUST me, my readers, that there will be Lions in your houses, too, if you listen too credulously to indolence and fear.

Enterprise and action are the sinews of success in business and greatness in character. The value of a man is not to be estimated by the possession of talents but by their use. He who can speak or write or labor, and is neither an orator nor an author nor a husbandman, I pity from my soul, and regret that though he has courage, yet is afraid of the Lion.

Sloth is one of the most timid personages I know; she haunts the pillow and she invites to the tavern. A young student wakes at five. The morning is frosty, but though Duty commands to rise, Sloth whispers "There is a Lion in the streets."

Many sots of my acquaintance would be more sober than my Deacon, were they not driven to drams by harsh creditors and scolding wives. Creditors that insist upon present pay, and wives of clamorous tongue, are undoubtedly ugly and growling Lions.

Spleen, or as she is now generally called, Hypo, is a lady of most delicate nerves and trembles at the very name of Lions. Like some old women who are afraid that they may be shot by a gun not loaded, Spleen, if assured that there was no Lion existing but in the deserts of Africa, would be positive that she heard one growl in the streets.

I know a melancholy man who turns pale if only a flock of harmless sheep bleat as they pass his door; his terrified fancy changes them into Lions. He inherits from healthy ancestors a robust constitution, eats roast beef with a relish, and empties his daily decanter; but apprehensions of the gout and apoplexy constantly haunt him in the shape of Lions.

Many honest people who are unreasonably averse to wild beasts are afraid that the world they inhabit will not continue a week. About a hundred years ago, those who are "full of notions" declared that the globe would be burnt by an incendiary comet. They even felt themselves scorched by its tail, and many a white

handkerchief was soiled by wiping anxious brows. But the globe
still rolls merrily round, neither roasted nor broiled by a comet's
fire; and we may laughingly declare that the comet-gazers saw a
Lion in the sky as well as in the streets.

In the middle of July, tired of composing my sermons, I walked
into the meadows and searched anxiously for shade. I saw a laborer with a wooden bottle at his mouth and but little hay made
at his side; his useless scythe hung dangling from the limb of an
elm. He could not mow, for his arms were relaxed by rum, and
he saw a Lion in the grass.

I am, or think myself, an invalid, and have a whim, the offspring of indolence, that some seasons are more favorable to composition than others. I had taken it into my head that this week
was too cloudy to write with clearness, and meant, like some ordained parsons, to vamp an old sermon. But I felt shame busy
with her red pencil at my cheek, and became persuaded that there
was no Lion in the streets which led to the office of my Printer.
I applied gaily to my task, and endeavoured to convince my readers that they may work in any street without injury from the lion.

XIX

"I perceive that in all things ye are too superstitious."

SUPERSTITION is not confined to religious belief. The apostle Paul employed it in its broadest sense, and the Lay Preacher, well knowing the extent of its influence, proceeds to exemplify how men of America, as well as of Athens, may be in all things too superstitious.

Having no farm but only a small garden, I cannot be styled Husbandman, the most honorable of titles, and therefore know but little of agriculture. But when I see a strip of ground with here and there a spire of very luxuriant grass growing on its edge, and wheat in the middle, like Joseph's seven ears of corn, "blasted and thin," I know that the owner dares not think for himself. Should you ask him why he sows grain instead of planting the potatoe, he tells you "his father and grandfather before him did so." Here, my readers, is an instance of a "superstitious" farmer; the example, even of parents, will not justify folly, and my neighbor, Lawyer Summons, will tell you that a bad custom should be abolished. The yeoman who manages a farm erroneously and continues superstitiously to sow by the way side because his father did, will soon have nothing but an empty garner for the officer to attach.

When a country physician talks about specifics to "sweeten the blood," and points his lancet to the collapsed vein of a coughing and consumptive patient whom he drenches with milk instead of beef juice, I shudder for the meagre wretch, burnt by a hectic and drained by a quack. I compare him to a state criminal in England, sentenced not only to be hanged but drawn and quartered, and regret that a useful member of society is murdered by a mode of practice in all things too superstitious.

A fashionable man, as the ladies call him, is more superstitious than those Indians who worship the Devil. A fashionable man who wears silk hose in winter and a thick pudding under his chin in summer, who risks a crick in his neck by wearing the cape of his

[41]

coat on his shoulders, and whose dangling knee-strings are social with every ragged nail they meet, is in every part and parcel of his dress too superstitious.

A young woman who thinks that frankness in speech is a vice of the heart, who laboriously shuns meeting the eyes of man as though, like a black snake, he would first charm and then devour her; who never calls breeches by their right name and scolds two hours when a case of bastardy is mentioned, I am certain would make a poor and profligate wife, being in all things too prudish and superstitious.

No people under the sun enjoy such rational liberty as the Americans, protected by a government mild and amiable. The man who acquired this fair inheritance by his sword, now maintains it by his prudence. All of my curious readers have heard something of his character, all my grateful readers reverence it. Even the old women of my village, after reading his manly and moral speeches, lay down their spectacles and declare "this Washington a clever creature." Now could credulity suppose that there could be found a solitary grumbler, in all things so weakly superstitious and so wickedly ungrateful as to affirm that our government was tyrannical and its President ambitious? But shame to the "tardy gratitude of base mankind," not only individuals but "clubs" and "societies" of Americans, "seeing that by him we enjoy great quietness," strive to calumniate our chief governour, to turmoil his government, and to cause us, in all political cases, to be too superstitious.

XX

"The fashion of this world passeth away."

MORE quickly, in the Preacher's opinion, and in the milliner's practice, than the remembrance of a guest that tarrieth but an hour.

Those slaves to the mode who, from leisure and fortune, are most capable of resorting to "Vanity Fair" to learn and ape the fashions of this world, have a harder task than the porter in town or the haymaker in the country. A new coat every month and a vest of a different pattern every hour are hardly sufficient, in the opinion of a jury of beaux, to excuse a man from presentment for high treason against the law of taste.

Customs, the lawyers affirm, to have validity, must be equally old and certain. Customs which I copy, says the coxcomb, must be as changeable as the silk gown, or the temper, of a mistress.

St. Paul, who, I believe, never visited Paris, appears rather hostile to fashion's freaks, although in many respects he was of a very complying character. In one of his epistles he makes particular mention of the ladies and their dress, but is so uncouth and austere as to allow them only three suits, which he calls by the barbarous names of shamefacedness, sobriety, and good works. These uncourtly terms I lately asked a woman of fashion to define. With the volubility of her sex she first railed at poor Paul for presuming to dictate in dress, and then told me that they meant linsey woolsey and grogram, flimsy manufactures, fit for none but Jewish chambermaids to wear.

If one of the patriarchs could get up out of his grave and survey the chins of his descendants, he would not fail to conclude that the race of man was annihilated by another deluge and that the daughters of Eve had the exclusive right to the globe. The fashion of this world regulates our persons no less than our garb. Fashion cherishes a length of hair at one time, and snips it at another. An antediluvian, in his tent, would encourage his beard to sweep his breast. A modern coxcomb at his toilet will pay a barber to keep the beard shaven. In the days of Cromwell and puritanism, fashion settled the length of countenance as well as the width of conscience. None but long-visaged penitents could be numbered among the elect. In the merry days of Charles the Second and the profligate, behold the opposite extreme: the features of levity contracted by laughter and all faces as short as the Spectator's. We read in ancient British history that King Richard and his courtiers chained their shoes to their knees; whoever marks a modern fine gentleman tripping along the street will discern that his shoe-chain is attached to the instep and has dwindled from ponderous silver or gold to airy black ribband. The history of whiskers has been so copiously detailed by my brother parson, Sterne, that I am almost excused from another paragraph. But whiskers have had their fashions, and suddenly have they passed away. The gallants in Shakespeare's days used to consider them as ornaments of the cheek, and "by my mustachios" has been the courtly oath of a Spanish gentleman. Whiskers were then unaccountably worn, not as the pink of taste but as the insignia of valour, and degraded by German corporals and hussars into scarecrows to terrify the enemy. This is not the last of whisker revolutions. Within a few years a smirking race called, in fashion's vocabulary, "Tippies," reassumed whiskers, and their pallid cheeks, thus accoutred, exhibited a surprising compound of ghastliness and effeminacy. But the scythe of the mode, at length, has nearly swept these superfluous hairs away from the face, and what weed will next grow there must be left to some future scoffer against custom to record.

When I began this sermon upon the vicissitudes and vanity of fashion, I marked down sketches of the alterations in female dress as a distinct topic on which I should enlarge as became a preacher. But this was too vast an undertaking for a writer so concise as myself. Besides, the limits of my discourses are too narrow for such an immeasurable theme. Far from being compressed into a single column, the things which should be written concerning the shop and box of the milliner would overflow a volume more ample than Ridgley's body of divinity, or the everlasting paraphrase of Gill. For the time would fail me, and it absolutely fatigued the long-winded Isaiah to tell of the change-able suits of a woman, of the hoods, the veils, the mantles and wimples, the bonnets, the head bands, and the round tires, which, the Prophet adds with a degree of wit you would not expect from his character, were "like the moon," incessantly varying like that planet. The ladies are the legislators of fashion, and their laws are so numerous and so often repealed, it is presumption to at-tempt a digest. But instead of exercising their ingenuity upon caps and gowns, the mode of which passeth away, would they study more durable graces and make the white robe of neatness, candour, and modesty fashionable, they may be assured it is of such admirable texture that, like certain old brocades, it will not only look but wear well, and be "in season all the year."

XXI

"The fashion of this world passeth away."

AS I am only a *Lay* Preacher, it must not be expected that I should always exhibit that accuracy of sermonizing which characterises the settled pastor. But having observed, in the course of a long and regular attendance of public worship, that divines are in the habit of dividing their matter and of adjourning, sometimes, the morning exhortation till after dinner, I thought it expedient, when I selected the fruitful theme of last week's meditation, to reserve part of its topics till now. For, during the process of critically examining my subject in all lights, I found that fashion regulated speculation no less than practice, and that opinions, as well as dresses, had their times and seasons. As we are told, by a profound reasoner, that as there is but one sun in the natural so there can be but one truth in the intellectual world, an abstract metaphysician in his cell would suppose that by this time, that *one* truth was discovered and hence, necessarily, induced uniformity of thinking. But this is a mere reverie of a novice in the history of man. In theology, in the healing art, in politics, in the fine arts, and in polite literature, in whatever interests, in whatever amuses our species, perpetual vicissitudes occur, and what is supposed to be settled by one party at one time is unhinged by different theories at another.

In the infancy of the colony at Plymouth, and at the erection of the Saybrook Platform, our emigrant forefathers rejected with loathing the fat luxury of Luther and starved themselves on the mean fare of Calvin. They were doubtful even of scriptural truth if it had issued from the Clarendon Press, and would not read the Sermon on the Mount to edification, unless imprinted in a Bible at Geneva. Willard's body of divinity was their law and testimony, and reprobate was that sinner who would adventure to read and practice a more gentle and generous system. But such heavy and clanking fetters of the mind were too irksome to be long worn patiently by fretful sceptics, and infant Catholicism, in its cradle, at length ventured innovation. Good works were sometimes associated with implicit faith, and the piety of our primitive Christians was not always horror-struck at the union. In process of time the reign of rigor declined, and now it may be said the high prerogative of superstition has become as nugatory as kingly power in France. For a new dictator in divinity who knew not Calvin, arose; and Chauncy, considering brimstone as a Scottish or an old wife's fable, proclaimed salvation to *all* men, and insisted that a profligate should not be eternally singed for his sins. Hume and Bolingbroke, with elegance and elaboration, but with the darkest sophistry, and Boulanger, an audacious Frenchman, in his *Christianity Unveiled,* have presumptuously attempted to sap the Christian's fortress and now to represent the son of Mary as a mere man, and now as an imposter. These writings have induced flimsy opinions called, from their nature, deistical, to predominate; and their professors, far from consulting the editions either of England or Geneva, will inspect no Bible. Perhaps the accurate reader will pronounce my enumeration incomplete unless I notice that second edition of Tom Thumb's folio, called *The Age of Reason.* But as this, in mechanic's phrase, is but a bungling vamp of obsolete infidelity written by a drunken author, rarely quoted except by the lowest vulgar and then in the lisping accents of intoxication, I will not condescend to an analysis but terminate this head of my discourse with the warmest wishes that, in spite of jarring opinions, Gospel charity and benevolence may be everlastingly fashionable, and that men will not expect a more excellent mode from the new-fangled looms of Paine and of Paris.

Physic has experienced more revolutions than Poland, or even France, since the Capets are no more. Boerhaave has prescribed at Leyden what Brown would reject at Edinburgh. Gout must be pampered according to one physician, and starved by another. The small pox, like Sancho Panza, is sometimes blanketed into submission and sometimes every wintry wind must be invoked to blow the infection away. Dr. Cheyne insists that his patients shall quaff a perpetual bowl of milk, while a more jolly physician directs as perpetual and much ruddier draughts. Le Sage's Sangrado drained every vein, and now every vein must be inflated like a bladder. Cullen departed from Boerhaave, Brown has exposed and abjured the heresy of Cullen, and probably by this time some European projector has started a new theory, to the utter destruction of the old.

A logician, considering the two subjects as equally variable, would infallibly class weathercocks and politics together. We behold vast empires sometimes governed by a solitary woman, and petty states headed by a mob of rulers. Kings, once ranked with gods, are suddenly and capriciously degraded among felons.. Government, as a nervous writer expresses it, is sometimes scandalously relaxed and then violently stretched beyond its tone. The Corinthian capital of society, laboriously erected by aristocratical artists, is prostrated by popular fury in an hour. In our own country, political modes are perpetually fluctuating. Prior to the formation of French friendship, that people, their religion, and their politics, were equally detested. The Pope was Antichrist, the French King his high Steward, the government of France was the archtype of Turkish despotism, and the nation viewed as a motley collection of coxcombs and slaves. Mark the instant operation of a single defeat on the whole political sense of America! A captured Burgoyne could metamorphose an arbitrary Lewis into the friend, the patron of republicans. But the love towards Lewis soon waxed cold, and Marat had his proselytes here as well as at Paris.

Very suddenly have most of our political fashions past away. Britain has been called a mother, a hag, a sister, or a fiend. Our rulers are perpetually wrangling concerning the garb of government. Some, from Geneva or Virginia, affect the broad mantle of republicanism, which covers a multitude of sins. Others prefer French manufacture of the Paris cut. A few, perhaps, wish to import materials from England, but there is a good, warm, well-made, easy garment, made to fit any one, called Federalism, which the Lay Preacher actually prefers to his canonicals, and prays may be constantly worn, and an unchangeable mode.

XXII

"Issachar is a strong ass."

WILLING to carry any burdens through thick and thin, the dirtiest roads, the most formidable obstructions, the "hill difficulty" or the "valley of humiliation" are all the same to the "strong asses" of this world.

On my return from a visit to a brother parson I stopped at an inn for refreshment, and an African hostler held my stirrup for a weary limb to dismount. His hat was under his arm, his body bent to more than a curve, and his looks of cringing obsequiousness for a moment angered me, not at him, for I saw *slave* in the furrows of his cheek, but at the first Gold Coast navigators who thus dared to change humanity into a "strong ass." Not slaves alone are thus meanly subservient, I observed to myself. I know some in that predicament who are free. Is it possible? How free? Why, they have the keys to their chamber—they go like the winds where they list—they are not in the custody of the officer—but avarice sends them on vile errands, and to fetch or carry gold they "couch down," like Issachar, the "strong ass."

I sometimes see a little mercenary attorney "couching down" at the bar, taxing his bill of cost and pointing to the careless client that he has forgotten "one shilling more for this writ." I hear him argue—not with ingenuity, not with eloquence, for then I should do him homage—but by rote, croaking sentences from the statute book and hesitating law from his "puddled" memory. I hear him scold a trembling culprit as a toothless old woman scolds a wayward child: a culprit for the first time, whose only offence is cutting a twig from the wayside tree. But this urchin avenger of public wrongs holds his dogs-eared law in one hand, and rudely pushes from him "*sweet mercy*" with the other. His bray, his stupidity, his callousness are all derived from the house of Issachar, and when I see him with his green bag, moiling for the last dollar of the entagled client, verily I see as "strong" an "ass" as the Patriarch did when he gazed at the most sluggish of his children.

THE LAY PREACHER

On some of those days when I do not preach myself, I sit down in the body seat of the first meeting house that I find. Occasionally I am instructed by an ingenious sermon, modelled by a "workman that needeth not to be ashamed," but when the clergyman is corpulent, red faced, and a heavy leaner upon the cushion, when he sounds divinity through his nose, when he copies the huge pages of Dr. Gill, or Flavel, and reads them without emphasis, though I cannot discern long ears rising each side of his wig, I am confident that some "strong ass" has mistaken the pulpit for a stable.

When a candidate for Congress, instead of studying the Constitution at home, is constantly in a bar room, with a mug of flip in his hand, courting the suffrages of the populace; when for the sake of a vote he resigns his best-grounded opinions to slide easily into those of his neighbour; when, like Absalom, he stands at the city gate, taking every stranger familiarly by the hand, inquiring his grievances, and hinting that, "If I were a ruler in Israel how soon they would be redressed," the most careless elector may anticipate Virginia politics, hotter than the sun, battles against the funding system, crude calumny against the President, zeal for French lanterns, and resolutions of democratic clubs, enough to fill both panniers of "a strong ass."

Should I, in a morning's walk or ride, stop for rest at some log house or cottage in my way, and see a scurvy-looking fellow, smelling strong of nauseous drugs, poking frequently into old saddle bags for phials and feeling pulses which keep time with the watch, I should naturaly think of "Issachar." But should I hear the words "white swelling," or "right rose cancer," although I was a thousand leagues from the Cape de Verds and Spain, I should be positive that I heard something bray, and that some quack was near me in the shape of a "strong ass."

XXIII

"The heart of the foolish is like a cart wheel."

IF this be the fact, and the wise man accurate in his similitude, what myriads of wheels roll in this, our rolling world!

As it is the privilege of preachers to paraphrase their text and extort meanings that will slide easily into the train of their own sentiments, I shall choose to understand the word "foolish" as not only intended to indicate weak, but giddy and unstable men. This definition being granted, and it is not so far fetched as many which my fellow labourers John Flavel and Matthew Henry have framed, what greater affinity can be found between two things apparently unlike, than a hypochondriac writer and a cart wheel? Such a splenetic author as the Lay Preacher, for instance, restless, and whose labors are in regular rotation, moves through the ruts of life, creaking and complaining of obstructions in the way, and when the daily drudgery is done, is left, by the inattention of mankind, without a shelter, or sunk into a slough.

A very ancient moralist, who published his wisdom in the reign of Queen Elizabeth, introduces somewhere in his works an aged sire complaining of the clandestine nuptials of his daughter. As the height of his misfortune, the disappointed parent laments that his darling should espouse a fickle foreigner and, as it is expressed in the quaint style of that age, "Tie her fortunes to an extravagant and wheeling stranger." A romantic adventurer, continually shifting his situation, exposed to the temptations and vices of various regions, and, like the dove of Noah, perpetually seeking and never finding a settlement, must be grossly deficient in that uniformity of character necessary to the happiness of marriage. Be on your guard, therefore, ye parents, when your daughters are solicited to wedlock by those who are commonly called unsteady men, lest haply ye find them wheeling. The heart of a husband that is like a cart wheel will, in some of its unaccountable and wild rotations, be turned away from its duty or affections to the wife.

[51]

THE LAY PREACHER

Advice to women must be supposed most disinterested in the Lay Preacher. The reasons are obvious; he has, in a former sermon, hinted that he was full of years; and, moreover, from the gravity and restraint of his profession, cannot approach even the female cheek but with the salute of a saint or the kiss of charity. He therefore entreats the daughters of the land not to confound prudery with virtue, not to follow with too strict observance the changes of fashion, nor to be too ambitious of the artifice of coquetry, for all these things assimilate a woman to a wheel, whirling at a prodigious rate.

There is more hope of a fool than of that various creature commonly called a universal genius. Eager for novelty, and a stranger to perseverance, he goes on from one project to another, from art to art and from science to science, round and round like a cart wheel. In the younger part of my life I knew a man of the above description; I think his name was Schemer. If he happened to hear a veteran colonel talk of the siege of Louisbourg, he would buy military books and dream of drums and trumpets. In the midst of these warlike preparations he received a letter from his brother, a lawyer, informing that he had gained his great land cause at the last superior court. Schemer sold his cartouch box and read law for—two days. Jaded with the obscurity of this study, his restless mind demanded something new, and he listened with delight to the tale of an East-Indian captain who painted the profits of factorship and the brilliancy of "barbaric pearl and gold." In short, for to recount all his labors would tire even the long-winded Jeremy Taylor, he spent his life in ceaseless changes. He had at different times horses saddled for journeys to every part of the continent, and the departure of many an outward bound vessel was delayed by this projecting passenger. I lived with him a month and witnessed the variety of his pursuits. He might be found, in the morning, busy to invent some short cut to the temple of science; at noon he would be examining the wheels of a watch, and at night making a mouse trap. His life was the perpetual motion, and his palpitating heart and whirligig head were, in very deed, like a cart wheel.

XXIV

"Why stand ye here all the day idle?"

HAVING sauntered away a whole week in parochial visitations, the habit of indolence grew so strong that, on the morning of publication, my sermon was untouched, and the Deacon and I were lolling, with folded arms, against my study wainscot. The printer entered the room, asking for my copy; when he saw my paper without a character traced on it and my study table covered, not with texts but tobacco, he sarcastically exclaimed, "Why stand ye here all the day idle?"

"Truly, Deacon," I responded, "this is a puzzling question, harder than knotty arithmetic which tormented my patience at school." Why stand we here all the day idle? Moments of relaxation are necessary, and we have them in abundance, but to stand, yea, and to sit and to loll whole hours and summer days idle, is a privilege which should never be asked by mankind. Let the sloth and the dormouse sleep, but let man be "up and doing." Each has a soldier's task to fulfil, and if neglecting the front of day we ignobly skulk in the rear, the tour of duty will be unaccomplished, and we shall, sorrowing, hear the voice of some moral sentinel crying, "the night is coming, wherein no man shall work."

It is almost presumption to attempt sketching even the outlines of indolence, since Solomon, the best character-painter in Jerusalem, has drawn a striking likeness of the sluggard and has shown what a silly figure the man makes who "stands all the day idle." I have gazed whole hours at this pretty picture which the wise man exhibits and am persuaded that it is better worth ninepence of any man's money than a sight of the lion now carrying about in a cage. But as lazy folks will not even read little story books, much less the Bible, I know of no better mode to teach them self-knowledge than by designing a modern sluggard in miniature and hanging it up in the first column of the Walpole paper which, it is said, even yawners read.

Dick Dronish lies in bed till eleven o'clock in a May morning.

Slip shod, and with one stocking wrong side out, he gapes over his breakfast, which he eats with "unwashen hands" because he can't afford to hire a servant to hold the water bowl. As his profession requires study, it is his duty to read all the forenoon, but he always sleeps over his book and never displayed any vivacity in study except once, when he threw Dr. Franklin's works into the fire for saying that "time was money." After dinner, which generally employs two hours, he cracks nuts like a squirrel or smokes like a Dutchman, or, by a certain process commonly called whitling, covers his hearth with shreds of pine. At four you see him exerting all his energies, crossing the street to a dram shop and loading a sot's pistol—with brandy. You need not enter Dick's house to become acquainted with the proprietor. You see him through the broken windows and know that the rusty hat which supplies the lost pane belongs to the head of an idler.

Not only individuals but sometimes whole tribes and bodies corporate "stand all the day idle." I once journeyed through a certain town whose inhabitants, as I was credibly informed, like some animals described by naturalists, passed the whole year in a state of lethargy. You might hear them snore as they sauntered through the streets, and a witty friend observed to me that there the common forms of salutation ought to be changed, and that two people, when they met, instead of asking each other "how they did," should ask how they slept, or whether they had pleasant dreams! At Clumsy College, where I had my education, governors and pupils stood for the most part idle. The heads of the college were sometimes lifted up when some braying dunce vociferated his declamation, but "the still small voice" of genius rarely interrupted their learned repose. To such a drowsy education the candid reader of these discourses must attribute the tediousness and insipidity of the Lay Preacher.

XXV

"They made me the keeper of the vineyards, but mine own vineyard have I not kept."

THIS is the frank confession of Solomon, in one of the stanzas of his "Song of Songs."

During some moments when he enjoyed a respite from pleasure in his voluptuous harem, the wise king might inquire by what strange fatality he had been raised to a throne and pronounced wise, when some of his appetites were so grovelling and some of his actions so foolish. My readers will not, I think, require me to quote Josephus, or the Jewish Rabbis, to prove that Solomon sometimes departed from the dignity of a prince, and did not always display the judgment of a philosopher.

As we know from his excellent treatise entitled "The Preacher," and from the three thousand proverbs which he spake, that he was occasionally, at least, in the habit of thinking soberly, I feel assured that, although he did not choose to encumber a song with much sentiment, the following was the soliloquy which occasioned the text of this sermon.

'By the partiality of my subjects, and their implicit belief of the excellency of my wisdom, I have been made keeper of the vineyard or, in other words, monarch of Israel. My fame has reached distant nations. I have the reputation of possessing more knowledge than all my contemporary philosophers—than Ethan, and Heman, and Chalcol and Darda. The botanists assure me that I speak learnedly of trees, and that I describe the various genera and species of the vegetable kingdom, from the aspiring cedar to the lowly hyssop. Hiram extols my skill in mechanics and affirms that not an architect throughout the realms of Tyre can rival the ingenuity of my designs. My subjects praise the blessings of my administration. Foreigners and travellers vie with each other in making their court to me; every man brings his present of what is most valuable, vessels of silver, and vessels of gold; even the caprice of a female has, for once, been restrained, and the Queen of Sheba's admiration of my wisdom was the same when she left as when she entered my palace. But do I completely deserve these various and enthusiastic encomiums? Have I well governed myself, as well as my kingdom? Have I noted and corrected my own faults with the same circumspection that I remarked and punished those of other men? Am I not obliged, conscious of the license of my own palace, to suffer the men of Judah and Israel to waste all their time eating and drinking and making merry, and is not this revelry the pernicious result of my careless example, rather than a chastized joy under my prudent government? Have I consistently arbitrated with rigor the differences between two harlots, while seven hundred are quarreling in my seraglio for the lawless favors of their sovereign? No, even myself, endowed with superior powers, have often proved weak and wicked. Placed upon wisdom's summit, I have descended; forgetting my dignity, thoughtless of my duties, prostituting my throne, I have been ravished with strange women and have drunken of the wine which the sons of riot mingled. I have been promoted to the highly responsible office of keeper of the vineyards, but mine own vineyard I have not guarded vigilantly.'

If Solomon could walk with so good a grace through the valley of humiliation, which we are assured, on the faith of Bunyan, is one of the most rugged rambles that a Christian can take, surely in these modern and degenerate days, almost every man who is a keeper, either of vineyards or anything else, may inquire whether he has at all times been a faithful keeper to himself. For if, as we read, that man who has been faithful in a few things shall be ruler over many things, to what office shall that man be appointed who neglects his own duty? Few can be found who would not, in the hour of self abasement, discover that such was their weakness or their wanderings, they had not strength enough to till the vineyard or stability enough to remain there.

One of the poets who did not, like the rest of the tribe, always delight in fiction, after recounting the sage precepts of a certain philosopher, adds,

"That, strange to tell, he practis'd what he preach'd."

Notwithstanding my absolute conviction that a pastor ought to be an ensample to the flock, I have no doubt but that I, sometimes, vary from my own doctrines and negligently keep my own vineyard. I warmly hope that my readers will gather grapes from my thorns and, when they peruse my exhortations against drowsiness, that they will not inquire how long I court the morning pillow.

XXVI

"Yet no man remembered that same poor man."

IN the book of Ecclesiastes we find related in a very familiar and simple apologue the siege of a certain city. It was little and thinly inhabited, but it was invaded by a powerful king and menaced by mighty bulwarks. Instant capture must have ensued had not a certain poor man, whose mind was better stocked than his purse, delivered, by the wisdom of his plans, the city, and freed the inhabitants from their terrors. Here we naturally anticipate a lively picture of the gratitude of the besieged towards this political saviour. Too many statues could not be erected in honour of such gallantry and enterprise, too many shekels of silver could not be given to relieve the poverty of him who had so well deserved. We might suppose that the wealthy citizens would pay liberal tithes to one by whom their all had been saved. Chaste dames and coy virgins, exulting that their purity had not been violated by a licentious soldiery, would naturally crowd around their protector and the blushes of a thousand cheeks attest that modesty had not been injured. But he who should draw this conclusion and imagine that even useful poverty must necessarily be recompensed, would prove himself a rash and unobserving man. We might allow the benevolence of his own heart, but what should we think of his knowledge of the hearts of others? That men are not always grateful for signal favors, that poverty is ever contemptible even when accompanied by merit, may be learned in the course of every day's experience, may be learned from the sequel of the story which began this sermon. Though all men, natives of the besieged city, had such occasion to recollect their benefactor, yet the mortifying conclusion of the narrative is that, in the words of my text, "no man remembered that same poor man!"

However penury may be disdained by those selfish ones whom legacies and avarice have enriched, we find that the best friend of man abounded in benedictions of the poor. In the Sermon on the Mount, a much more accurate and eloquent discourse than any of Masillon's, the poor in spirit are especially named and a kingdom promised them, surpassing all the thrones and principalities of Europe. It was not the magnificent palace, it was not the usurer's bank—it was the poor man's hovel, it was the recess of the forlorn outcast, which the son of the carpenter visited. To the poor the Gospel was preached; it was a poor widow whose two mites shone more brilliantly in the eyes of one not likely to be dazzled, than all the gold of those opulent contributers who cast in much to the Jewish treasury. The rich man, querying concerning future life, is told that a sale of his possessions and liberal donations to the poor are essential to salvation. While wealth and power and rank were neglected, poor shepherds enjoyed the honor of a glorious annunciation. The companions of the son of Mary were not the opulent pharisee and the Roman patrician, but the poor fishermen of Galilee. When dispatched to exercise the functions of apostleship, they were forbidden purse or scrip. The wealthiest of them was worth but thirty pieces of silver, and those Judas gained by speculating upon his Saviour. The close of the bargain might prove that poverty was better than riches. His title to the cash proved more rotten than a Georgia purchase. As he was hanged for his pains, his money raised him for a time, but then "it was fifty cubits higher than he dreamed of."

XXVII

"Gad, a troop shall overcome him, but he shall overcome at the last."

THE patriarch Jacob, in his last moments, having summoned his sons to hearken unto his prophecy and to receive his benediction, after characterising their temper, proceeds to describe their future fortunes, and emphatically observes of Gad that though at the first onset of numbers he would be vanquished, in the end he would prove a victor. This singular prediction was doubtless justified by the early habits and undaunted perseverance of the heroic son of Israel. The observing patriarch had remarked the conduct of Gad in some scene of adversity. When the tempest of misfortune loured, he did not, like unstable Reuben, run for shelter to his "father's couch." When the corn of Canaan was blighted and the rest of the children of Jacob looked anxiously one upon another, he did not despair of making an easy Egyptian purchase and of filling their sacks from the granaries of Pharaoh. I think I can see him on the road to Egypt, looking forward, confident and determined, not murmuring, like his fellow travellers, that the famine was so sore they should certainly perish, but cheerfully exhorting not to despond, and expressing his animated hope that either the hospitality or avarice of the country would furnish them subsistence. While the irritability of Simeon and Levi, inflamed by hunger, was manifested by angry execration; while Issachar, no more an ass couchant, brayed loud discontent, and Naphtali, careless of his wonted plausibility, forgot to give goodly words, the perseverance of Gad was unbroken and the philosophic serenity of his temper unruffled. He felt the pressure of hunger as a man, and therefore could not whimper like a child. "Shall I make," he might say, "the same simple bargain as my uncle Esau? Shall I lose my courage when it is most useful, in the hour of necessity, and sell my spirit for a morsel of bread? No! although the ovens of my country are empty and there should be no herd in my father's stalls, although not a lamb shall be left me to fold at Sechem and the fairest of our olives refuse her fruit, if I must perish, let me perish like a brave man, and let death find me not meanly prostrate, but in an erect posture."

Few of the youthful personages in sacred history challenge our admiration more than this gallant son of Zilpah, whom the discerning prescience of his father saw would prove finally superior to every obstacle of ill fortune. I confess, in my familiar style, that I love the character of this primitive lad of spirit; I wish his example to be faithfully copied by aspiring youth, and that, when eager to behold rising merit I look through the lattice, I may behold a troop coming, and of the tribe of Gad.

A pagan philosopher, although he never heard or read a word concerning Jacob or his sons, yet was so pleased with a character similar to that pourtrayed in my text, that he breaks out into a most passionate exclamation of praise, describing

"A brave man struggling with the storms of fate,
And greatly rising . . ."

and concludes, with the enthusiasm peculiar to his age and country, that to discern such a spectacle the gods look down anxiously from their skies.

When I see a worthy husbandman ministering affectionately to the distresses of his family, stretched on sick beds in every room of his cottage—when I hear him tell the sheriff, attaching the last of his kine, that he hopes better times when he can discharge honest debts without legal compulsion—when I see him persevere to labour in spite of bad crops, and cast repining cares behind him, I think I see a hero and a sage, and that, though a troop of sorrows harass him now, he shall, he will, overcome them at last.

A youth whom I observe at work betimes, and in the intervals of leisure reading books of instruction; when I remark farther that he is not capricious in business but the same yesterday and to-day, that he quits the beaten track of authority and hearkens to the suggestions of his own mind, often telling him more than seven watchmen sitting above in a high tower, when I hear his neighbours say he is prudent, patient, and persevering, it will not stagger my belief if they add that, like the angel of the Laodicean church, he is "poor and miserable, blind and naked," for I am positive that he will overcome at last.

XXVIII

"On the first day of the first month--set in order the things that are to be set in order."*

IT has been remarked by ingenious moralists that although the negligence of mankind suffers minute divisions of time to pass unregarded away, yet at the close of centuries or years it is common to pause and compute in what manner they have been employed. To justify the truth of this observation, most of my parishoners who have toyed with time, days, and months, begin now to grieve that another idle year is gone and resolve that the next shall be more busy. While all around him are repeating the compliments of the season, and with jocund voices wishing each other "A happy new year," the Lay Preacher, with affectionate zeal, will suggest plans by which these annual wishes for felicity may be realized.

Most men are criminally idle. I confess with candor that I loiter and slumber much, and while I preach industry to others, am myself a castaway. But the sun, which darts his reproachful rays through the curtain undrawn at nine o'clock, seems to upbraid my sluggishness and to wish that I would announce to the lazy of my flock that they will not, like him, at once shine and be of use, unless, like him, they rise seasonably. My readers are therefore vehemently exhorted early to extinguish their candles and to use the Day Lamp, which neither sputters nor flares, whose wick never burns out, and whose oil never fails. All who wish that the year may be happy must rigorously observe this injunction. No complaints must be heard of the chill of winter mornings or the shortness of summer nights, but as soon as the above Lamp begins to glimmer, let them rise and work. They will soon be convinced that it is so ingeniously contrived its radiance will not offend the eyes nor its exhalations taint the lungs, like the vulgar tapers of midnight. If the Lay Preacher himself should,

---

* *A New Year's sermon.*

contrary to his own doctrine, be found snoring in his study while his neighbours are walking in their vocation, he gives them full permission to call a council and dismiss him from his office.

Instead of employing the usual expression of "A happy new year," it would, perhaps, be an improvement to vary the phrase and adapt it to the character of the person who is addressed.

Thus, should I compliment a man of feeble knees, whose eyes are red and whose purse is impoverished by "tarrying late at the wine," I should wish him a sober year. I should wish that his landlord, when the third bowl or bottle is called for, would refuse to trust, and that the liquor he swallowed, instead of raising, would depress his spirits, and that he might peruse seriously that chapter of the Prophet which denounces "woe to the drunkards of Ephraim."

If I meant that a sluggard should enjoy a happy year, I should wish him an active and laborious one. I would apply to some noisy teamster or some importunate client to bellow at his window at the dawn of day. I would even advance a dollar from my small salary to purchase a couple of cocks to crow him up to exertion. The year of the idler would then undoubtedly be happy. You would hear from him no complaints of spleen or nervous disorders. He would have no bill to pay the apothecary for pills to cure indigestion. He would not only "set his things in order on the first month," but habit would cause order to appear throughout his affairs during the year.

Suppose that I should tackle a sleigh and go with my wife to Boston. I could not fail, either in the market or some coffee house, of meeting that animal, more restless than a humming bird, called a Democrat or Jacobin. If I wished him a happy new year, he would instantly conclude that I meant a revolutionary one. He would imagine that my wish involved the abdication of Washington, the execution of Jay, and the introduction of the Guillotine. Now, as I am a good subject and perfectly well satisfied with the present order of things, nothing could be farther from my intention. Guarding against a meaning so mischievous, I would express my annual compliment differently, and wish him an obedient and well governed year. I would interdict him from reading French gazettes, forbid his pronouncing the word "Robespierre," and debar him from nocturnal clubs or speeches. The man would infallibly become a good federalist, and his year would be happy.

The wish for gamblers must be expressed in a very extraordinary and enigmatical manner. Instead of a *happy* new year, it would be the duty of their real friends to pray that it might be an *unlucky* one. An unlucky year would be a year of jubilee to the gamester. Such a year would operate a thorough reformation. Should the friendly wish for ill luck be realized, and the gamester neither hold pam flush, four by honors, nor the odd trick, what a clear saving to his purse, his health, and his time! He would soon consider cards as the emissaries of misfortune; he would endeavour to grow rich by surer calculations; he would not only discard the Knave from his hand, but from his conduct, and be more anxious to turn the penny than a Trump.

Finally—to use the Parson's immemorial adverb—finally, brethren, the Lay Preacher, with the fervent kindness of St. Paul, "sendeth greeting to many" and wishes that this and every future year may prove eminently happy. That this hope may not be deferred, he recommends the adoption of every laudable mean to promote so valuable an end. Due attention to order in the distribution of time, to economy of expense, and to prudence of behaviour, will occasion the present to be like the happiest of past years, yea, and much more abundant.

XXIX

"For lo! the winter is past, the rain is over and gone, the flowers appear on the earth, the time of the singing of birds is come, and the voice of the turtle is heard in our land."*

MEN who have witnessed the horrors of that tempestuous and deformed season which, by its cold contracts the body and by its gloom depresses the mind, naturally feel, at the first glimpse of warmth and vegetation, an undescribable rapture. Even in the mild climates of the East, in the sunny gardens of Palestine, the slight, the short and fleeting winter was considered an enemy to joy; and Solomon congratulates the arrival of Spring in a strain of uncommon gaiety. In a tone soft as the season and animated as its pleasures, he exhorts his "fair one" to "rise," to "come away," and in the open fields to hear the wild music of nature and to observe her green and tender tribes bursting from the sepulchre of cold. This invitation is enforced by a most lively description of the landscape; and the appropriate metaphors Solomon employs seem inspired by the very genius of the season, and the liquid and harmonious words he selects are responsive to the turtle's notes.

If a native of Jerusalem could be thus elated at the succession of spring, after the mildest reign of winter, what must be the delight of him who, under our northern skies, beholds for more than half the year a waste of snows, hears the midnight howl of the storm, and feels the nitrous needles of a frigid atmosphere, lacerating every pore?

But suppositions are superfluous. We need only look at the door of the cottage, or stray into the nearest pasture, to discern the operation of spring upon the hopes of the husbandman. Tired

---

*Published the first of May.

of the dull and sullen company of the austere months, and disgusted with the chimney corner which denies room and exercise to his plough, at the whistle of the first robin he flies like "the roe" or the "young hart of Bether," to furrows and fields. The genial sun burnishes his manly cheek, the soft and voluptuous air vivifies his sturdy limbs, he surveys the rising blade and anticipates the golden harvest.

But though Nature in her various exhibitions of verdure and of flowers and by her chorus of singing birds, seems, at first view, to have no other object than to amuse our species, as a painter or musician, yet, on reflection, we shall find her both a provident matron in preparing our nutriment, and a useful monitor urging us to toil. As I am entirely of opinion with that ancient and with that poet, who saw his duty inscribed on every leaf and found a tongue in trees and books in the running brooks, I think it would not be unprofitable for every man who looks abroad, to remark that every department, both in the animal and vegetable kingdom, is in action. Those countless tribes which, during winter, were fast locked in the chambers of frost, are now each moment on the wing and incessantly employed. No pause can be discerned in Nature's present operations; every energy is awake, and even inert matter increasing. It seems to me impossible that an idler should rove on our mountains and not be lessoned into industry. In January, when green corn could not wave and the violet of our valleys was folded, he might argue himself into a belief that, to him, a suspension of native powers was alike necessary. But in May, there is a million incentives to exertion, and not one reasonable excuse for supineness. Man was destined to activity, like the other parts of our system, and they call on him to lend a helping hand to their labors. The most minute drop of sap rising in its tube, and the embryo germ bursting from bark, to a contemplative listener appear to speak and upbraid the slothful man for not being in useful motion like themselves.

The parallel has been so often run between the spring time of the year and the spring time of life, that all remarks and doctrines upon this resemblance must be, of course, trite and elementary. But though the theme is by no means novel to my younger

readers, I wish them to permit me, for once, to forego all attempts
at originality and to add a hundredth remark to the ninety-nine
of my predecessors. They will gratify the Lay Preacher if amid
their rapid career of thoughtlessness and pleasure they will stop to
make some provision for the dreary season of old age, which will
inevitably find that stores of some kind are necessary. They will,
I hope, sow the seeds of wisdom seasonably and not, like the fool
of Lord Bolingbroke, plant in autumn and expect to reap in winter.

XXX

"And she made haste, and let down her pitcher from her shoulder, and said, Drink, and I will give thy camels drink also."

FROM my attachment to simplicity in writing, I read Sterne more attentively than Stackhouse and prefer a story in Genesis to a volume of Gibbon. It appears to me, that notwithstanding the sarcasms of Voltaire and other French infidels, that mode of writing which finds a ready way to the heart was never more successfully achieved than by the orientals. The other evening, as I was turning over, agreeably to my usual practice, the pages of scripture, I dwelt with undescribable pleasure upon certain passages in the life of the patriarch Abaham. I had passed the afternoon in what is called modish company, and yet could not avoid remarking that the extreme selfishness of men and women of the world led them, even at a moment when they assembled for ostentatious civility, to behave discourteously. If such rudeness, I murmured to myself, can be tolerated in a refined age, let me view the behaviour of those of old time, before dancing masters were discovered and when message cards were not sent by one patriarch's lady to another. I found, as I expected, that even herdmen and shepherds had as much genuine politeness as Lord Chesterfield, and that a country maiden, the daughter of Bethuel the son of Milcah, could behave with as much propriety as though she had been educated in a boarding school. The story of this pastoral girl's conduct I wish to tell at large, and that the delicacy of fashionable readers would allow me, on this occasion, so much pedantry as to quote the original. But as a whole chapter in Genesis might appear too long and disproportionate for a short sermon, I will attempt to narrate in my own words.

Abraham, a most affectionate parent, perceiving that his life

declined, and zealous with the anxiety of old age for an establishment for Isaac, entreats a confidential steward of the household
that he would not suffer the inexperienced heart of his son to be
captivated by the Canaanitish beauties. At the earnest request of
the Patriarch, the servant binds himself to solicit for Isaac a wife
of his own rank, religion, and country. After sanctioning this
promise by one of the most tremendous oaths among the Jewish
usages, he harnesses his camels and departs for Mesopotamia. On
his arrival at the suburbs of Nahor, a city of that country, fatigued
with a tedious journey and tender of his drudging camels, he makes
them kneel by a well of water to take their necessary refreshment.
In this weary moment, Rebekah appears; and the first accents that
fell from the parched tongue of the traveller were to solicit a little water from the pitcher which she carried. "And she made
haste, and let down her pitcher from her shoulder, and said,
Drink, and I will give thy camels drink also."

Let us now gaze earnestly at these simple yet beautiful features.
The female whose courtesy is thus recorded was a woman of
some distinction in those pastoral times. Her father was of a
stock abundantly respectable, for he was allied to Abraham, and
her brother was the opulent Laban whose cattle strayed on a
thousand hills. Engaged in domestic duty, she meets a stranger,
in the garb probably of a hireling, for he is called in the text
"servant," begrimed with dust and having no claim to her favor.
She is asked for water, which she cheerfully gives, and the careless
reader will not be aware of the extent of the obligation if he have
not surveyed a map of Palestine and adverted to the sandiness and
thirst of the soil. In that arid region a brook was a more joyous
sight to a panting shepherd than a bumper to the votary of wine;
the invaluable well-spring, eagerly sought and obstinately con-
tended for by different tribes, was, from the nature of the earth,
at such a distance below the surface that to obtain water was a
work both of toil and time. But forgetting her home, forgetting
herself, and "disdaining little delicacies," she thinks only of the
sufferings of the wayfaring stranger; and with that "kind charity" which the apostle emphasizes, with that genuine, disinterested
civility, beyond the court of Versailles, the tedious descent of the

well she repeatedly tries, and the cooling pitcher imparts not only to the man but even to his unpetitioning beasts. "Drink," says the generous girl, and, trust me, I can feel likewise for your burdened companions, "for I will give thy camels drink also." This was benevolence such as is not generally found. It was eminently disinterested, prompt, and diffusive. It was disinterested, for the tongue which she cooled was not that of a youthful gallant trolling the oily phrases of flattery. He who drained the pitcher which the assiduity of Rebekah filled, was an old man, a servant, and a stranger. It was prompt, for she "hasted," and she "ran" to do good, and drew water for "all the camels" though the troop consisted of ten. It was diffusive, for *they* were minutely regarded no less than their proprietor.

I warmly wish that the manners of many who deem themselves polished were, at the present day, as excellent as those of this primitive well-bred woman. Frequenting no assemblies but those of the next green or meadows, receiving no lessons of good breeding but those which her own warm heart dictated, we find her deportment graceful, though she never paid a dancing master; we find her a maid of honor, though she never saw a court! True politeness, unlike that of men of the mode, consists in actually rendering little services to our neighbor, rather than in the ostentatious promise of great ones. Indifferent to its own ease, it thinks much of another's, discerns the latent wish, and supersedes the necessity of asking favors by seasonably bestowing them.

XXXI

"Watchman, what of the night?"

TO this query of Isaiah the watchman makes, I think, but a simple reply, and tells the Prophet what, if he had the least smattering of astronomy, he must have well known before, "that the morning cometh, and also the night." Any old almanac could have said as much. I think that night, however sooty and ill-favoured it may be pronounced by those who were born under a day-star, merits a more particular description. I feel peculiarly disposed to arrange some ideas in favour of this season. I know that the majority are literally blind to its merits; they must be prominent, indeed, to be discerned by the closed eyes of the snorer, who thinks that night was made for nothing but sleep. But the student and the sage are willing to believe that it was formed for higher purposes, and that it not only recruits exhausted spirits but sometimes informs inquisitive and amends wicked ones.

Duty, as well as inclination, urges the Lay Preacher to sermonize, while others slumber. To read numerous volumes in the morning, and to observe various characters at noon, will leave but little time, except the night, to digest the one or speculate upon the other. The night, therefore, is often dedicated to composition, and while the light of the paly planets discovers at his desk the Preacher more wan than they, he may be heard repeating emphatically with Dr. Young,

"Darkness has much divinity for me."

He is then alone, he is then at peace. No companions near but the silent volumes on his shelf, no noise abroad but the click of the village clock or the bark of the village dog. The deacon has then smoked his sixth and last pipe and asks not a question more concerning Josephus or the church. Stillness aids study, and the sermon proceeds. Such being the obligations to night, it would be ungrateful not to acknowledge them. As my watchful eyes can discern its dim beauties, my warm heart shall feel, and my prompt pen shall describe, the uses and the pleasures of the nocturnal hour.

Watchman, what of the night? I can, with propriety, imagine

this question addressed to myself. I am a professed lucubrator, and who so well qualified to delineate the sable hours, as
"A meagre, muse-rid mope, adust and thin."
However injuriously night is treated by the sleepy moderns, the vigilance of the ancients could not overlook its benefits and joys. In as early a record as the book of Genesis I find that Isaac, though he devoted his assiduous days to action, reserved speculation till night. "He went out to meditate in the field at the eventide." He chose that sad, that solemn hour, to reflect upon the virtues of a beloved and departed mother. The tumult and glare of day suited not with the sorrow of his soul. He had lost his most amiable, most genuine friend, and his unostentatious grief was eager for privacy and shade. Sincere sorrow rarely suffers its tears to be seen. It was natural for Isaac to select a season to weep in, which should resemble "the colour of his fate." The darkness, the solemnity, the stillness of eve, were favorable to his melancholy purpose. He forsook, therefore, the bustling tents of his father, the pleasant "south country" and "well of Lahairoi;" he went out and pensively meditated at the eventide.

The Grecian and Roman philosophers firmly believed that "the dead of midnight is the noon of thought." One of them is beautifully described by the poet as soliciting knowledge from the skies in private and nightly audience, and that neither his theme nor his nightly walks were forsaken till the sun appeared and dimmed his "nobler intellectual beam." We undoubtedly owe to the studious nights of the ancients most of their elaborate and immortal productions. Among them it was necessary that every man of letters should trim the midnight lamp. The day might be given to the Forum or the Circus, but the night was the season for the statesman to project his schemes and for the poet to pour his verse. Night has likewise, with great reason, been considered in every age as the astronomer's day. Young observes, with energy, that "an undevout astronomer is mad." The privilege of contemplating those brilliant and numerous myriads of planets which bedeck our skies is peculiar to night, and it is our duty, both as lovers of moral and natural beauty, to bless that season when we are indulged with such a gorgeous display of glittering and useful radiance. It must be confessed that the seclusion, calmness, and tranquility of midnight is most friendly to serious and even airy contemplations. Milton, in one of his poems, says fervently,

"Let my lamp, at midnight hour,
Be seen in some high lonely tower,
. . . . To unfold
What worlds, or what vast regions hold
Th' immortal mind, that hath forsook
Her mansion in this fleshly nook."

The rigid Dr. Johnson was so convinced that late hours were auxiliary to the feast of reason and the flow of soul, that he used to declare, "No man but a scoundrel went to bed before midnight." This expression was, perhaps, too strong, and he would not have used it had he lived in a farmhouse. But his love of the conversation of men of letters, and his experience that Fancy is generally most wakeful when Dullness sleeps, tempted him to employ a phrase which must startle every laborer who, by mere lassitude of limb, is compelled early to retire.

Night being friendly to playful no less than to metaphysical and abstract thought, not only the author and statesman watch, but likewise the sons of sociability and glee. Those who "eat the bread of carefulness" go soon to bed to digest their meal, and leave the darkened hours to be enjoyed by men of genius or wasted by men of pleasure. St. Paul avers that they that be drunken are drunken in the night, and I know that its broad mantle is frequently employed to cover excess from the world. Still, the arrival of night is greeted by many who wish neither to sleep nor drink it away. Conversation often holds a levee at midnight, and Wit, Sentiment, and Song, like the fairies, assemble and sport before the cock-crow. I think it treason to this sable power who holds divided empire with day, constantly to shut our eyes at her approach. To long sleep I am decidedly a foe. As it is expressed by a quaint writer, we shall all have enough of that in the grave. Those who cannot break the silence of night by vocal throat or eloquent tongue, may be permitted to disturb it by a snore. But he among my readers who possesses the power of fancy and strong thought, should be vigilant as a watchman. Let him sleep abundantly for health, but sparingly for sloth. It is better, sometimes, to consult a page of philosophy than the pillow.

XXXII

"Better is the end of a thing, than the beginning thereof."

ASSUREDLY, says I, with a desponding face, when I dipt my pen into my ink-horn and expected to bring up a sermon from the bottom, my little flock of readers expect that the Pastor will make his weekly visitation; and yet I feel too languid to excurse far. I wish that the task was fulfilled; verily, verily, Solomon, whether you muttered it when building the temple or thinking of your concubines, you never muttered more wisdom than "Better is the end of a thing than the beginning thereof."

Without an invocation to the sons and daughters of Indolence, for we all know what would be the language of that family, should even the persevering and industrious be asked the question, they would refer the querist to Solomon's works for an answer.

Beginning, continued I, is like John Bunyan's hill, so difficult that it would embarrass even a Christian to get fairly over. Beginning! why it is the terror of schoolboys and of pretty Miss in her teens; it makes lawyers stammer and lovers timid. I hate to *begin* my sermon; and, quoth my grandmother, looking at her knitting work through spectacles, "I would rather foot ten pair of your blue stockings than *begin* one."

But of *ending,* how many fine sentences could I scribble, had I "the pen of a ready writer!" How exultingly the Saint talks of "finishing the faith," how cheerfully the labourer swings his scythe when haymaking is done, and how briskly a bridegroom ascends three chamber stairs at once when courtship is at an end. I married a fond couple last week and, as usual, neglected the wedding sermon till the eager twain came blushing into my study. When I joined their hands, I felt pulses beating high through their white gloves and saw eyes sparkle expressively when I extemporized from "Better is the end of a thing than the beginning thereof."

One of my parishoners, a very industrious and thriving cobler, who supports a wife, "nine small children and one at the breast," by his labour of leather, I knew "even from his boyish days." At fourteen he sang wicked ballads to his fellow apprentices, drank raw rum, in a frolic, out of the old shoes of the shop, and burnt the boots of the customers. At twenty-one, three benevolent maidens complained of him to the Squire, and he was obliged to pawn his freedom suit to indemnify the parish. He next commenced a roaring blade, drank flip before breakfast, laid out his heel-tap money in tobacco, and the tavern clock struck one when he told the last negro story. At length he picked up Dr. Franklin's "Poor Richard" and found that this was not "The way to wealth." He broke his mug, threw away his box, bought stock, earned money, kept it, and married. I stopt at his shop a few mornings since, at sunrise, to try on a pair of shoes. As soon as the noise of six of his journeymen's hammers ceased, I could not forbear comparing the past with the present. "Ah," said I, looking wistfully at his last and the waxed thread he was twining, and thinking that St. Gregory, St. Austin, and all the fathers of the Church have punned, "Ah, Mr. Crispin, how much more profitable is your end than your beginning."

Paley, an archdeacon of the church, and what is much better, a worthy man, tells us in his book of philosophy that there is a great difference between beginning with a thousand pounds and ending with a hundred, and the reverse. It is of much more import, therefore, if we mean to end well, that we should begin tolerably. I know no better beginning for a young man than a stock of honesty, prudence, and industry; it is better than stock in the shop or a thousand pounds from a rich father. If a man should take it into his head to begin with knavery and theft, it cannot be dissembled, though the words of Solomon are against me, that there are ignominious ends, and if hemp grew in Jerusalem he ought to know it; if not, I proceed to inform him that a rope's end is one of the most pitiful terminations in life. Neither better nor best can be predicted of such an end, even by the accuracy of his logic. 'Tis a vile end, and, you trickish jockeys, be not in such haste to put off your spavined horses for double their worth to the believing buyer. Lame as they are you may be willing to avail yourselves even of their imperfect speed to convey you to the Genesee. Better that the lake fever should be your end, than the gallows.

When my spirits are the victims of the east wind, when one of my agonizing headaches disturbs the "palace of the soul," when my small salary is scantily and grudgingly paid, or when remembrance of false friends' ingratitude presses strongly upon me, I then read the third chapter of Job and exclaim, "Better is the end of life, than the beginning." Some there are who are perpetually crowned with rose buds of delight, before they are withered, who "eat and drink, and enjoy the good of their labour," and then "rise up to play." To this class, existence has abundant charms, and their airy fancies, pleased with the beginning of life's day, put far away the end. But it may be made a very serious question whether the majority would not pronounce the words of the text as a creed. He who is poor or miserable, blind or naked, must certainly wish for better accommodations, where he could be well paid, fed, and enjoy "perfect vision." To such an unfortunate, such a smoky house as he inhabits must be offensive; and if you convince his reason that in a "house not made with hands," more airy and gladsome apartments are prepared, his feelings will rejoice when his mortal lease expires, and he will apply and believe the above quoted words of Solomon.

XXXIII

"Quench not the spirit."

FOR should you, ye insensible ones, you would perhaps put out a light to lighten the nations. The lustre of spirit is brilliant, and even its heat is cherishing; let this fire from heaven, therefore, be never obscured, lest darkness overshadow the land and thick darkness the people. Let him who is largely furnished with the gifts of mind, not only have his merit seen, but rewarded; and in obedience to the precept of Paul, let the world fondly foster his active spirit. For if it prove a spirit of enterprise or invention, how will that world rejoice to behold it, like the hero of Milton, shooting upwards, a pyramid of fire.

My readers must excuse the preceding rhapsodical and glowing paragraph, so foreign from the usual level style of the Lay Preacher. The noble nature of the mind naturally renders one, supposed to have the care of souls, eager for its advancement and grieved at its depression.

"Quench not the spirit!" What an apparently superfluous caution! At first a careless, unreflecting critic might suppose that the phrase was employed by the saint of Tarsus as a rhetorical flourish to allure the attention of Agrippa or tickle the ear of Felix. "Quench the spirit," he would exclaim; why, who is there that would put that light under a bushel? I will tell thee, thou vain reasoner, and vindicate the saint. The neglectful, undiscerning world that suffers talents to lie in the napkin. Paul both felt and saw the necessity of such a serious warning as the text. Doubtless, while he was preaching in the forums of Rome or the churches of Thessalonica, he experienced the negligence of some and the ingratitude of others. He dreaded lest even his own fervent spirit should be damped, perhaps quenched, by the frowns of Caesar or the hand of a centurion. He felt that the supine lethargy of paganism could not be roused, even by the energy of his eloquence. He recollected that, determined by exteriors, the hasty Corinthians caught not the spirit of his doctrines and undervalued his mind because his body was weak and his speech contemptible. Conscious of the homage due to intellect, and sorrowing to behold the pearls of wisdom trodden under foot, he pertinently advises the Thessalonians, as in the text, not to quench the spirit, not to suffer genius to pine in obscurity.

Some years ago, in the capital of New England, a certain literary lawyer stood up, not to tempt but teach his townsmen. The desperate debtors of his native state had endeavoured to interrupt the course of its justice and crush the wheels of its government, and he historicised the events of the insurrection. While I was on the form of a Latin school I recollect studying a narrative of a conspiracy at Rome, written with singular purity by Sallust. I think, and politer scholars than a Lay Preacher are of similar opinion, that if Sallust could have been summoned to record the revolt of Shays, he could not have produced a work frugal of words, prodigal of ideas, happy in expression, like the volume of the lawyer. But it seems that his fellow-citizens wanted a Paul to caution them, for they would not defray the charges even of binding the book. They quenched the spirit of the historian. Eager to know the cause of such criminal lack of patronage, in my last journey to the metropolis I traced many a street and lane in quest of genius. I looked, and lo! a modest man, neither a French philosopher, nor a dancer on wires, nor a vaulter upon steeds, nor a writer in the "Chronicle." Ah, I muttered to myself, if the flame of his spirit has not blazed in these directions, it is not marvellous that the cautious Bostonians should cry "Quench!"

XXXIV

"I hear that there be divisions among you, and I partly believe it."

IN the social state obviously framed for the promotion of the common good, a credulous man might suppose that there would be no divisions. But this mistake, Observation, if she had only half an eye and peered with that through a glass darkly, would correct. Where only two or three are gathered together, some unsocial, malevolent passion will start up and forbid their unanimity. But in great and political bodies, among old and rival nations, opinions being as numerous as the individuals who harbor them, there the clash of faction and the clash of swords will be so often heard that there will be no room left to doubt "divisions."

I believe that I have, somewhere, hinted to my readers that a newspaper lies occasionally on my table. But I survey that weekly map of human life, more with the feelings of a moralist than of a politician, and shed tears rather than wine at the intelligence of a victory. If the public papers recorded the happy marriage and not the sudden death, if they painted the tranquility of a *Federal* and not the turbulence of a *French* government, every son of sensibility would peruse them with rapture. But, especially at this jarring period when our ears ring with "the world's debate," it is most painful to turn over pages which, crowded with recitals of battles, sieges, assassination, and slaughter, are nothing more than the records of animosity. The old world is rent in pieces by "divisions." Nothing but "wars" and "fightings" can satisfy the restlessness of France, the pride of England, and the stately ambition of Germany. In France there is jangling in the Cabinet as well as the shock of hostile lances in the field. How many wise and virtuous men have felt the edge of a Revolutionary ax because they differed in sentiment from a Revolutionary Tribunal. How many Britons have found untimely death in the dykes of Flanders, who might have been gathered like a shock of corn in his season, had not "divisions" among the nations urged them far from peace and the plough. However men may talk of universal benevolence and the amiableness of the charities of life, yet we hear every day of division among them, and we are forced fully to believe it. In our own country, though the weapons of war are sheathed, yet "divisions," frequent and pernicious, like the tares and thorns in the parable, arise and mar the peace of the community. Among the borderers of Pennsylvania, "Division" touched with a brand the head of the whisky-still, and the fiery spirits of insurgency blazed against a government the first and fairest on the earth. Division has been the president of many a "club" and "self-created society,"—Division, a scowling monster more ugly than the "Green Dragon" whose den she was wont to haunt. Division has looked askance at the Treaty and has even with audacious front adventured to assail Washington, but he steadfastly smiled, and she vanished away.

Men disagree and divide in minute no less than in momentous questions. My parishoners inform me of various divisions, and I partly believe them. Thus I hear that two young girls of equal pretensions to wit and beauty cannot possibly live in friendship together, for, like the Caesar and Pompey of Lucan, one cannot bear a rival and the other is impatient of a superior. I hear that two neighboring shopkeepers will not even look at each other nor go to the same tavern, nor walk the same side of a street—all in consequence of an unlucky division. Two counties will contend for years which shall enjoy the privilege of a shire and where the Courthouse shall stand, and thus cut out work for lawyers, even before a place is provided for them to wrangle in. Neighbors will squabble about an old tree and an old horse, and expend 100 dollars in court fees, to determine which shall have the mighty privilege of putting out the fire by piling on the wood of the one, and of having a neck broke by riding the other. But what is a more preposterous division than any enumerated is what is called an ecclesiastical dispute. To such an absurd height has this species of contention been carried that, in despite of the opinion of the Saint that a believing wife may convert an infidel husband, church doors have been shut against a converted female for pairing with an unconverted mate. Last of all, to end this disgusting catalogue of "divisions," Christians professing to worship in concert have pulled each other by the beard in ascertaining who should be their minister, and have warred furiously to know where the temple of peace should be erected.

XXXV

"Wine and new wine, take away the heart."

AND cloud the head, and empty the purse, and beget writs of attachment and an intimacy with deputy sheriffs and gaols; and —I should become quite out of breath and "the time would fail me" to recount all the mischiefs which wine and new wine occasion.

But I hear young Clod, my neighbor's hired man, whisper to the schoolmaster of the village, "Our grapes are sour grapes, from which we cannot press new wine. You cannot get a drop in New England except what the traders sell, and that comes over sea and is mingled with molasses in the vessel, and when it reaches us becomes new cider, rather than new wine." Now young Clod, having ploughed our uplands and chopped wood in our forests, and read Morse's *Geography*, has some right to conclude that the "hearts" of Americans cannot be taken away because we lack wine and new wine and experience not when the time of the vintage of the grape is near.

But the wise prophet who sang to the men of Judah, many hundred years ago, the many woes of wine, though he used that word, meant "intoxication" in its broadest sense. Had Hosea lived in New England and seen our laborers lifting a tin measure to their mouths at five o'clock in the morning, swearing at noon, and staggering at night, he would doubtless have prophesied that new rum, yea, and gin sling and brandy grog "take away the heart."

Hear me, my countrymen, I am not an Universalist nor a New Light, but I am a *moral* preacher. Though I do not whine to you from a pulpit and have not the voice of the charmer charming never so wisely, yet I have your good at heart and will promote it all in my power; and I ask no salary but your reformation.

You complain that lawyers oppress, and that Congress tax you, that you have no money, that you must work hard, and that, though some of you wish to read useful books and pamphlets, you have not cash to exchange with the bookseller. I will hint that mode of conduct which escapes a bill of cost, supports government, makes labor light, and procures you a whole library. It will render you in very deed that virtuous and enlightened yeomanry which shall be the pride and protection of our empire.

You inhabit a region which, though it has not been celebrated by the poets, though its rivers are not so warm as those which feel a southern sun and roll through Italy and France, has a soil productive of all the essentials to health and happiness. The sharp air of your hills blows away disease, and your juicy beef is a better bracer than the bark. If you will plant the corn and sow the rye and wheat field, pay necessary debts and contract no superfluous ones, and drink wine and new wine, and rum and brandy, with moderation, believe me, you will have property enough for your occasions; you will not be haled before the judge, neither will the officer cast you into prison; but your barns will be full, your kind will, like Jesherun, "wax fat," and the shade of the prophet, if it hovered around you, might whisper, "Hearts like these shall never be taken away."

XXXVI

"One thing is needful."

ALL the readers of the *Farmer's Museum* thought so lately, when they snatched that paper from the post and saw not my Sermon. "What could induce the Lay Preacher to forego his wonted labours?" was the general exclamation. Various were the conjectures concerning the omission of my duty; and some of them resembled the pleasantry of the Prophet: that I was either talking, or pursuing, or on a journey, or peradventure sleeping and would not be awaked. My vanity being thus flattered by the inquiries and anxiety of my friends, I will frankly inform them that in the course of last week I read three excellent sermons, one hundred pages in Josephus, two of the canonical books of Scripture, and a leaf or two in the volume of the human heart, but *one thing was needful;* my head was clouded by care, my hands were slack to labor, and the spirit of invention had fled away. I therefore dismissed my duty, as Felix dismissed the accused apostle, to a more convenient season, and devoted the vacant hours to ease, endeavoring to compose my cough and my cares.

Although most modern authors, and some clergymen, choose to write without thinking, I am so whimsical as to be positive that it is the *one thing needful.* I shall never preach without at least two or three ideas in my mind, and as I live in an obscure corner of the world, have only half a dozen books on my shelf, and see but very few faces, my readers must not be surprised if I manage my brain as a prudent farmer his field: be satisfied with its produce at one season and allow it to remain fallow at another. The little stock of prudence and knowledge of which I am owner is very much at the world's service; and when I can say any thing new or useful I will do it cheerfully and employ my neighbor Carlisle's paper as my speaking trumpet. But when I am sick or stupid, I am resolved not to repeat myself or quote other men, merely for the sake of scribbling. Always in literature, and sometimes in life, originality is the *one thing needful.* I always seek for it as for hidden treasure, and when I fail to find this jewel of great price, miserable thoughts arise in my mind and muddy ink flows tardily from my pen.

But let me not wander too far in quest of apologies. I trust that my acquaintance with my readers has been so intimate that they feel the usual prejudices of friendship and are willing to excuse slight deviations, conscious that I am generally inclined to study many sermons, and to write a few. I hope that the spirit of indulgence abounds, and that Candor is so constant a companion as never to be the one thing needful.

Such is the wandering of desire, that not a mortal can be found so perfectly satisfied with his situation as not to wish it either new modelled, or mended, or enlarged. To this restlessness of temper one thing is constantly needful, and as the poet expresses it,

> "That cruel *something*, unpossest,
> Corrodes and leavens all the rest."

The boy is eager to be a man, and the maid a wife; the merchant must freight another ship, and the farmer purchase more acres, to render their respective felicity complete. But imaginary wants, the bastard progeny of inordinate desire, are not the one thing needful which the reprover of Martha enjoined. To forsake old follies and to cherish good affections is the genuine interpretation.

Why do you charge that simple, unsuspecting country lass two shillings and sixpence for a piece of your faded ribbon which would be dear at a penny, Mr. Sharp? Your answer is ready; you point to your money chest; you declare it is not yet full, and that money is the one thing needful. This is a great mistake, believe me; had you told me that honesty and good faith were lacking, I might have credited your story. But what need have you of money? You have neither generosity to impart, nor spirit to use it; it is dead matter in your hands; your bank bills are fresh as from the press of the engraver, and your dollars more discoloured with disuse than a rusty nail. Why do you cry incessantly to your customers, "Give! Give!" like the daughters of the horse-leach, and falsely insist that you are poor and that wealth is the one thing needful.

"Why do you assume that prim air, and sit with the stiff up-rightness of a maypole?" quoth I to a coquette whom I observed at church more studious of her shawl than of her prayer book, and gazing with more devotion at tall striplings than at the Parson. Oh, Sir, tomorrow is my twenty-seventh birthday; I must be quickly married; a husband is a necessary piece of household fur-niture; to an *old* maid, he is undoubtedly the one thing needful.

XXXVII
"Great is Diana of the Ephesians."

THE usual exclamation of prejudice, ignorance, or enthusiasm in every age.

In the Acts of the Apostles, the occasion of this phrase is pleasantly recorded. St. Paul and his colleagues, perceiving the absurdities of the pagan system, ventured to expose the futility of the heathen worship and to point out a better way to the heavenly country. But the manufacturers of idols, terribly alarmed at an innovation which would probably abridge, if not destroy, the profits of their trade, immediately convened, though not to deliberate but to dogmatize. For instead of reasoning coolly upon the subject, and attempting to prove to the populace the celestial origin of their goddess and the active concern she took in the affairs of mortals, they gave a loose to their passions, became full of wrath, and bawled out that Diana was *great,* without once showing why. Of all that hot-headed multitude, perhaps not an individual had geography enough to ascertain the site of Ephesus, or history enough to inform him of the adventures or exploits of Diana. Craftsmen had told the ignorant crowd a pompous tale, to allure them to the silver shrines, and they believed, without examination.

I heartily wish that this cry of enthusiasm had ceased with the superstition of the ancients. But noises of this nature still tingle in our ears, and a town clerk at the present day, like his temperate predecessor at Ephesus, could not walk in the market place out of hearing of "Great is Diana" or some other sound equally as ridiculous.

Whether it proceeds from the warm climate in which they live, or the brisk champagne they drink, I know not, but the French are singularly prone to momentary fits of enthusiasm, almost bordering on convulsions. They are a very voluble and clamorous race, and if they take it into their heads to like Diana they will swear, not without gestures, that she is *great,* though all others affirm she is *little.* Montesquieu might reason, or Rousseau might harangue, but the French would not hear if those sanguinary craftsmen, Marat and Robespierre, should summon them to the Convention or the Champ de Mars to assassinate a king or to destroy a government. Trifles like these would be "light as air" to a Frenchman if an insidious desperado bawled in his ears the greatness and the glory of liberty and equal rights. One unlucky day they set up a certain scowling image, denominated, in their pretty and liquid language, the Guillotine. This, to be sure, had a shrine rather of steel than silver, and bowed heads rather than bended knees were the modes of adoration. Those unlucky subjects who, during a life of loyalty, had been much in the habit of crying "Great is the King!" were soon offered up as a Jewish sacrifice, for times were changed and they should have said: "Great is 'the Mountain!' "

A degree conferred by a college is a Diana whose divinity many a dunce has acknowledged. College honors, as they are termed by the craftsmen, often operate like amulets and charms, and protect a pedant from the warfare of wit and ridicule. They are a species of salt which has saved many a weak and decaying brain from putrefaction. Not a graduate from Cambridge but vaunts of his Alma Mater and cries, "How prescient, how witty, and how wise is the University!" A sceptic might doubt the greatness of this our learned Diana. Its foreknowledge consists in predicting invisible eclipses of the moon, its wit lies at the bottom of a syllogism, and its wisdom watches the weathercocks and compiles a bill of mortality!

Some have thought that the Cambridge Diana did not deserve to be worshipped by the learned world. I was once asked by an inquisitive foreigner, in what alcove of our University were deposited its own works. "It is agreed," says he, "that a College is designed to read and write in. Doubtless many of your professors were poets; among your tutors I expect to hear of a Cicero, and the invention of so elevated a character as a President must certainly have produced a folio in every science." My unbounded affection for the college where I had the honor to pay some three or four hundred pounds for instruction in the first elements of— nothing; my tenderness for the character of instructors of the most bland and accommodating humour; and my zeal for the literary renown of the most fashionable seminary in my country, urged my silence to this query of the stranger concerning a subject so delicate. Dear and learned Sir, I replied, the works of the University are not confined within the narrow precincts of an alcove.

THE LAY PREACHER

The works of the University, Sir, are seen, are seen—on Commencement days. They are diffused throughout—I wish I knew where, except in the form of stewards' bills, I muttered to myself. The gentleman, perceiving my hesitation and being a man of great curiosity and anxious to hear me quote brilliant couplets from some University laureat, or whole orations of some eloquent tutor, now insisted upon a categorical answer. I therefore, in a suppressed voice broken by many sobs, the tears running down my cheeks, and with a world of apologies, was compelled to reveal to him the nakedness of literature at Cambridge. To his astonishment, and to my sorrow, I narrated facts, "pitiful, wondrous pitiful," like Othello's sufferings. I informed him that the tutors, far from being eloquent like the orators of antiquity, were in general such raw boys that they were obliged to spell out even the stated prayer from the confused breviary of evening recollection. That the elaborate trifling of one professor was protracted through five lectures to show his pupils what a verb was—not. That another, in his divinity chair, would insult his hearers with the silly miracles of Polycarp, and in his public exercises purloin from Leland the materials of a funeral eulogy. That philosophy was pedlared out by the pennyworth, and the streams of learning, instead of being cheaply and easily conducted to each student, were sold, in their muddiest state, for a higher price than mineral water. That I never heard that any of the College Principals were ever poets or painters, or produced any work more meritorious than a Greek Grammar. That some were of such dubious taste as to reject from the College Library the works of Sterne and Swift, and to commence, at the age of fifty, the study of the British Poets as a task reading! I informed my friend that the best and brightest scholars, from Dr. Mayhew to the present time, were generally ignominiously punished for no other crime than that of volatility. I added that if any incorrigible dunce wished to hide his length of ear by a square hat academical, if dray-horses sought a shelter, or the King of Spain's fourfooted and braying subjects a dormitory, I could easily mark the place. But for a youth of lively parts and sanguine temperament, place him between the upper and nether mill-stone rather than on his knees before the leaden shrine of our Great Diana of Literature.

XXXVIII

"Yet did not the chief butler remember Joseph but forgat him."

A most unlucky instance of shortness of memory, and a strange one, too, for Joseph had expressly stipulated with the imprisoned butler that he should recollect the favorable interpreter of his dream and obtain from Pharaoh an order for his enlargement.

Forgat him! Is it possible? Did the chief butler, as he filled the cup to Pharaoh, taste the wine so often that it made him stupid or mad? Was the vine juice of Egypt ever mixed with poppy water that it might, like the fabled river of oblivion, drown memory and her tribes? As I know of no ancient record that alludes to this practice, and in the biography with which Moses has indulged us of the chief butler, not a syllable is said concerning his debauchery, I believe that the supposition that he was a toper must be waved. We must look a little deeper than the bottom of a glass, or even a bottle, to discover the source of a courtier's ingratitude.

Let us look, therefore, once more into the book of Genesis, and I trust that so lucid an historian as Moses will shed light upon this sombre subject.

It appears that Joseph, suspected of an attempt upon the virtue of Potiphar's wife, was, by the instigation of that harridan of antiquity, committed to prison. According to the sacred text, this was a state prison, a kind of Egyptian bastile where, as we read, "the king's prisoners were bound," where meaner fellows were excluded, and none were admitted but such courtiers and retainers to the palace as had, by their carelessness or their crimes, forfeited the royal favour. It is no great wonder, then, that a couple of tradesmen who had such frequent temptations to cheat, as a butler and a baker, should be put in ward. Light bread and sour wine had been vended in the palace, and the abused palate of Pharaoh was offended. Joseph, who had ingratiated himself with the chief gaoler, was appointed a sort of deputy, or turnkey, of the prison, and had the charge of these very delinquents.

One morning, "Behold they were sad;" and when interrogated concerning the cause of their gloom, they informed Joseph that they had dreamed, and there was no interpreter. The chief butler then related that he had seen, in a vision, a clustered vine of triple branches whose grapes he pressed into the cup and gave into the hand of Pharaoh. Joseph, after comforting the prisoner by familiarly explaining his dream and promising him restoration to his post in the household, pathetically beseeches him that he would, in his prosperity, reflect on his unjustly accused friend and mention him to his prince. "Think on me," says the beautifully simple original, "when it shall be well with thee, and show kindness, I pray thee, unto me, and make mention of me to Pharaoh, and bring me out of this house." This was surely an easy service; and, on the third day, when Pharaoh feasted his servants, when amid the jollity of an entertainment the released butler stood at the elbow of his appeased sovereign, what a favorable moment to suggest the propriety of loosing poor Joseph who had been so unjustly bound! But mark an obsequious, callous, courtly slave. Intent alone upon his own prosperity, he is so busy in filling the ruddy cup for his king and for *himself*, that not a thought of him intrudes who has nothing to drink but his own tears and the waters of affliction. A selfish and ungrateful man, though he should outlive the oldest of the patriarchs and allay the thirst of a lineage of Egyptian monarchs, would not once think of his benefactor, nor call to mind that visionary vine which he had seen in adversity. No, a chief butler would have much more lucrative employment than thinking upon the "sorrowful sighing of a prisoner." A chief butler did not remember Joseph, but forgat him.

Are there not a thousand worldly reasons for this forgetfulness? Prudence might whisper to the butler, as he walked through the prison gate, not to lisp the name of Joseph, for, possibly, it might anger Pharaoh, and then his favour would be withdrawn—and the butlership! Besides, we should remember that this dreamer in prison was a very courtier in the palace, watchful enough of his own and "dealing out his *promises* as liberally as his liquor." When Joseph had unravelled his entagled dreams and foretold that he should again have the keys of Pharaoh's beaufet and cellar, I dare affirm that the butler, with cringing complaissance, with low bows and perpetual smile, engaged upon his honor not merely to remember but to remunerate his deliverer. This was the promise of a courtier. And who is ignorant that his engagements, like "your humble servant" at the bottom of a challenge, mean, if they have any meaning, nothing but death and destruction? Many are the promises of the chief butlers, the Chesterfields, the smooth-tongued men of the world. They *keep* them, too; but so close, that when the day of performance arrives, not even their owner can find them—mislaid in some obscure corner of memory's chest!

THE

LAY PREACHER.

BY

JOSEPH DENNIE.

COLLECTED AND ARRANGED

BY

JOHN E. HALL, Esq.

COUNSELLOR AT LAW.

PHILADELPHIA:

PUBLISHED BY HARRISON HALL,

AT THE PORT FOLIO OFFICE, NO 133, CHESNUT STREET.

J. Maxwell, Printer.

1817

TO THE READER

To gratify the repeated demands which have been made in the public journals for some account of the late Joseph Dennie, Esquire, and a complete edition of his writings, the editor of this volume was urged by an affectionate regard for his memory. Gratitude whispered that the founder of the *Port Folio* should not be forgotten by his successor; and justice, calling to mind the ornament of society, the Columbus of polite literature in this hemisphere, the zealous friend and the elegant writer, seconded the amiable suggestion. During the summer months of the present year, the editor sojourned among the friends of the deceased, that he might learn the story of his life. He tarried in the villages and questioned the inhabitants of the metropolis of New England. By such means he accumulated a mass of materials which must be interesting to those who love the memory of Dennie and are curious on the subject of domestic literature. Among other papers, his familiar and his literary correspondence alone would form an article unusually attractive. But it is mortifying to confess that the neglect which uniformly attends every effort in this country to vindicate the claims of "lettered worth," unless it has been blazoned in a foreign clime, urges the editor to remember the cautious conduct of Cumberland, who tried his *Observer* in an obscure village. In a similar spirit, dictated by that species of necessity which compels a man to consult his judgment rather than his heart, the present volume is confined to a narrow compass, and the edition is restricted to a few impressions. If it should be well received, some hazard may then be encountered. But during the rage for English books which now prevails, maugre our hatred, malice, and uncharitableness towards that country, it would be worse than folly to offer the life and writings of an American author to a community which purchases with eager avidity the most disgusting details of English profligacy,* and regards with indifference the classical beauty, the gorgeous eloquence, and the sound sense of an Ames, a Hamilton, and a Harper.

Philadelphia, 1816.

---

*The Editor alludes here more particularly to the rapid sale of "The Book," the "Life of Lady Hamilton," and "Glenarvon; a novel."

PREFACE

As the title of this work may appear ludicrous to some and be obscure to others, as many start at the word Preacher, and may sneer at a Layman tampering with theology—it is proper to state this is not a volume of sermons. It is a series of essays, modelled after the design of Addison and the harmless and playful levity of Oliver Goldsmith. The mottos are copied from the oriental writings; but they are either a moral lesson, an economical precept, or a biographical picture. The topics to which they are prefixed are didactic, descriptive, or airy, as the gravity or the humour of the hour prompted. On the fenced and walled and hallowed ground of religion, the author has never presumed to trench, nor carelessly nor wantonly approach the confines of the regular clergy. The doctrine and discipline of the church are sufficiently and gloriously illuminated from many a golden candlestick; and the citadel of Christianity is well guarded by the lynx-eyed vigilance of Bishops Porteus, Watson, and Horseley. But a young man, sequestered and studious, imagined that the moral doctrines and the literary beauties of the Bible might be familiarly illustrated in vehicles cheap and popular. "On this hint he spake," and volunteered in a village as a Lay Preacher, without even "the laying on the hands of the presbytery." The author will soon respectfully appear at the bar of public opinion; and, in the impressive words of the ancient law, "stand upon his deliverance," nothing doubting of a fair trial from the discerning and candid and catholic—and careless of the crude criticisms of the malignant vulgar.

I

Design of the preacher

"I will rise now and go about the city, in the streets,
and in the broad ways."—*Song of Solomon* iii. 2.

IN a walk so wide and various, the pondering preacher, perhaps, can moralize upon the shifting scenes more profitably, aye,
and more pleasantly too, than a more heedless pedestrian. He
who sallies out for the express purpose of speculation and remark,
with his scrutinizing spectacles on and "with a patient ear," can
note and describe, with greater accuracy than the individual who
is cramped with the crowd or who, engrossed by some worldly
care, is hurrying onward to his object.

I have long been of opinion that if I could traverse the market
place, visit the mart, lounge at the coffee-houses, and explore, in
the homely phrase of Sancho, "every creek and corner" of a great
city, that I could profitably compose a little essay, and tell occasionally what I had seen and heard. With this opportunity, eagerly sought and long denied, I am now indulged. In the metropolis of my country I have found a sort of parsonage, which has
been my shelter for more than a year. Having had time to visit
many of my new parishoners, to compose my cares, and put my
study in order, I have thought it expedient to shake off sluggishness, to rouse from the dreams of abstraction, and to resolve, as
it seems Solomon, in my text, has done before me, to rise now and
go about the city, in the streets, and in the broad ways.

Many years ago I stood in a rustic pulpit and was wont to address myself to the few villagers who thought my sermons worth
listening to. It was literally "the voice of one crying in the wilderness," for the forest was frequently my study and my principal
hearers a gurgling brook, a silent valley, or an aged tree. I had
but few of the fathers to consult, and perused the best of books,
not with Poole's, but my own commentary. My discourses, like
the tedious narratives of farmer Flamborough in the "Vicar of
Wakefield," began to be "very long, very dull, and all about myself." My hearers grew desperate, and I disheartened. I took an

[97]

affectionate leave of them, migrated to the city, and sought preferment. Of the difficulty in obtaining it I quickly had occasion to meditate in the text of "Ye shall seek me, but ye shall not find me." Disappointed in my golden and romantic expectations of a benefice, I have become quietly submissive to the mandate of necessity; acquire, as fast as I can, "the knack of hoping;" and, like some cheery practical philosopher that I have read of, "draw upon content for the deficiencies of fortune."

But, though not translated to a see, nor even made chaplain to a bishop; though I neither snore with fat prebends in a stall, nor gloriously wake with a Watson or a Horsley, yet, as happy brides are wont to say, I have some reason to be pleased with the alteration of my condition. My study is enlarged, and I have received salary enough to purchase the works of St. Austin and a bible of better print than the little Scotch edition I used to twirl over in the country. Though the tithes of a Lay Preacher are very tardily collected, yet the more liberal parishoner does not always forget that "the labourer is worthy of his hire." Cheerfulness keeps pace with Patronage, and though there is not much danger that she will be outstripped by her companion, I have such good spirits and such agreeable reveries in my "journeyings," "whether from country to town, or "from Dan to Beersheba," that I often flatter myself I shall

"From diocese to diocese, to Canterbury pass, sir."

But enough of this levity. It remains to speak of the profit, or the pleasure, which I propose to my readers from my habit of going about the city. If, either as a watchman or a lounger, I traverse its streets, or its broad ways, the utility of such a ramble need not long be doubted. It will enable me to variegate my speculations, to discern all the hues of "many coloured life," to turn gay subjects to moral purposes, and furnish copious materials for rebuke or exhortation.

On the decisive authority of the sagacious author of the text, we are told that wisdom crieth without and uttereth her voice in the streets, in the chief place of concourse, in the openings of the gates, in the city. We are repeatedly assured, by one who perfectly knew all her haunts, that she standeth in the top of high

places, by the way, in the places of the paths, at the entry of the
city and at the coming in at the doors. Now, if such places be
her chief resort, it is surely laudable to look for her there, to go
about, and strive to meet her, and persuade others to be companions in such a stroll. This is an invincible argument in support
of the proposition; and if my readers, in their pride of logic, talk
of sophisms and fallacy, they virtually vote the words of the wise,
foolish; and Solomon himself, a simpleton!

II

On the Pleasures of Study

"Blessed is he that readeth."—*Rev.* i. i.

WHENEVER I reflect upon my habitual attachment to books, I feel a new glow of gratitude towards that Power who gave me a mind thus disposed, and to those liberal friends who have allowed the utmost latitude of indulgence to my propensity. Had I been born on a barbarous shore, denied the glorious privileges of education and interdicted an approach to the rich provinces of literature, I should have been the most miserable of mankind. With a temperament of sensibility, with the nerves of a valetudinarian, with an ardent thirst for knowledge and very scanty means for its acquisition, with a mind often clouded with care and depressed by dejection, I should have resembled the shrinking vegetable of irritableness, and like the mimosa of the gardens, have been doomed to be at once stupid and sensitive. The courses of nature and fortune having taken a different direction, parental benignity having furnished me with the keys, and discipline and habit having conducted me through the portico of education, I have ever found, whether walking in the vestibule of science, or meditating in the groves of philosophy, or hearkening to historians and poets, or rambling with Rabelais, such excellent companions that life has been beguiled of more than half its irksomeness. In sickness, in sorrow, in the most doleful days of dejection, or in the most gloomy seasons in the calendar, study is the sweetest solace and the surest refuge, particularly when my reading is directed to that immortal book whence the theme of this essay is taken. In an hour of adversity, when I have caught up this precious volume, I have found instantly the balm of Gilead and the medicine for the mind. The darkness of despair has been succeeded by the brightest rays of cheerfulness, and in place of grim phantoms I have found comfort, peace, and serenity.

I hope that this style of speaking occasionally in the first person will be forgiven, even by the most fastidious reader, when he adverts to the custom of my predecessors. A periodical writer can

hardly avoid this sort of egotism, and it is surely very harmless
when its employer muffles himself in the mantle of concealment
and in the guise, whether of a shrewd Spectator or a simple Lay
Preacher, walks unobstrusively abroad.   Mr. Addison and Mon-
sieur Montaigne perpetually indulge this habit; and on a very
careful inspection of many editions of their essays, I have always
found, by certain infallible marks, that those speculations had
been most diligently perused which abound in little sketches of
the manners, humours, and habits of their authors.   We are naturally curious thus to peep through the keyhole of a study, to see
a writer in his elbow-chair, and to listen to his story with the
fondness and familiarity of friendship.   Anonymous authors have
a prescription from Parnassus to paint themselves; and when by a
Tatler, a Spectator, or a Connoisseur, nothing but good colours
and modest tinting is employed, men look with mingled curiosity
and complacency at the picture.   In a speculation on the blessings
derived from a studious temper, if a miniature of a lover of books
is introduced, provided it be a tolerable resemblance and viewed in
a proper light, it will, by an easy association, lead the observer to
reflect more intensely upon the value of literature.

The utility and delight of a taste for books are as demonstrable
as any axiom of the severest science.   The most prosperous fortune
is often harassed by various vexations.   The sturdiest son of
strength is sometimes the victim of disease.   Melancholy will
sometimes involve the merriest in her shade, and the fairest month
of the year will have its cloudy days.   In these dreary seasons,
from which no man may hope to escape, sensual delights will
fill scarcely a nook in the gloomy void of the troubled time.
"Brief as the lightning in the collied night," this sort of pleasure
may flash before the giddy eyes, but then merely for a moment,
and the twinkling radiance is still surrounded with the murkiest
gloom.   Eating, drinking, and sleeping; the song and the dance,
the tabret and viol, the hurry of dissipation, the agitation of play
—these resources, however husbanded, are inadequate to the claims
of life.   On the other hand, the studious and contemplative man
has always a scheme of wisdom by which he can either endure or
forget the sorrows of the heaviest day.   Though he may be cursed

with care, yet he is surely blessed when he readeth. Study is the *dulce lenimen laborum* of the Sabine bard. It is sorrow's sweet assuager. By the aid of a book he can transport himself to the vale of Tempe or the gardens of Armida. He may visit Pliny at his villa, or Pope at Twickenham. He may meet Plato on the banks of Illyssus, or Petrarch among the groves of Avignon. He may make philosophical experiments with Bacon, or enjoy the eloquence of Bolingbroke. He may speculate with Addison, moralize with Johnson, read tragedies and comedies with Shakspeare, and be raptured by the rhetoric of Burke.

In many of the old romances we are gravely informed that the unfortunate knight in the dungeon of some giant, or fascinated by some witch or enchanter, while he sees nothing but hideousness and horror before him, if haply a fairy or some other benignant being impart a talisman of wondrous virtue, on a sudden our disconsolate prisoner finds himself in a magnifient palace or a beautiful garden, in the bower of beauty or in the arms of love. This wild fable, which abounds in the legends of knight-errantry, has always appeared to me very finely to shadow out the enchantment of study. A book produces a delightful abstraction from the cares and sorrows of this world. They may press upon us, but when we are engrossed by study we do not acutely feel them. Nay, by the magic illusion of a fascinating author we are transported from the couch of anguish or the gripe of indigence to Milton's paradise or the elysium of Virgil.

III

On Meditation

"Commune with your own heart upon your bed, and
be still."—*Psalms* iv. 4.

HAVING, in my last speculation, attempted to describe some of
the delights of study, in this paper it is proposed to consider the
true use of retirement.   Between them there should be a perpetual
alliance: nay, they are not only neighbouring and friendly powers,
but they are familiar connexions.   Amiable, interesting, and lovely sisters! if your worthy admirer be attracted by the riches of one,
he will quickly be delighted with the pensiveness of the other.
Study will give him all her books, and retirement conduct him to
all her bowers.   In no ramble will he experience more delight than
when he roves through the healthful wood or saunters through the
tranquil cloister, with retirement on his right hand and study on
his left.   Though their guise is exceedingly modest, though their
conversation has no resemblance to loquacity, though their best
attire is from no other wardrobe than that of sweet simplicity,
still they will always gain more regard from the wiser than all
the pageants of the pompous and all the plumage of the vain.

The royal psalmist, from whose divine odes I have transcribed
my text, was himself a memorable example of the utility of retirement, reflection, and self-communion.   It will be remembered
that he was a warrior, a statesman, a man of business, and a man
of the world.   In these various characters, though he often acquitted himself excellently well, yet unfortunately, in some flag-
rant instances, we perceive how much he was tainted by the infection of the world.   But when he shuts his eyes against the glare
of ambition and the gaze of beauty, when he ceases to touch the
harp of fascination and forsakes the cabinet and the camp, then
we recognize at once the scholar, the philosopher, and the poet.
In the strongholds at En-gedi, he is a mere soldier; in the palace of
Saul, a servile musician; in the cave of Adullam, a skulking fugitive; and in the forest of Hareth, an unhappy exile.   But when
he tore himself away from the thraldom of care, the bustle of business, and the din of Jerusalem, when he wandered away by the

brook of the field or the plains of the wilderness, when he retired to his chamber and communed with his heart, then he formed those noble associations and composed those exquisite performances, which will transmit his name with renown to the remotest posterity.

My Lord Bacon, Sir Walter Raleigh, Erasmus, Grotius, Mr. Addison, and Mr. Locke, together with a great multitude of illustrious men, have been deeply involved in the cares of public business as well as engrossed by the meditations of the closet. But for the fairest portion of their glorious fame, how much are they indebted to the latter! While the chancery decrees of Sir Francis Bacon moulder away in the hands of some master of the rolls, the experiments of his study and the essays of his wit, like certain exquisite paintings, grow brighter by time. While we peruse, with still renewing pleasure, Raleigh's history of the world, his unlucky politics are scarcely regarded. Mr. Addison was secretary of state, and Grotius an ambassador; but who inquires for the despatches of the one, or is interested by the negociations of the other? The fame of Erasmus, constantly immersed in the turmoil of his times and engrossed by cares, civil and ecclesiastic, would have perished with the names of those miserable monks whom he has derided, or those imperious princes whom he has courted. But by sometimes wisely withdrawing himself from the cabals of a court and the polemics of the church, by meditating on horseback and in his chamber, by avarice of time, by intenseness of application and ardour of genius, he has filled ten folios, composed in the purest Latinity, where an indolent reader can find nothing too prolix, and where a critical reader can discover nothing to reprehend. The foolish politics of Addison are scarcely remembered, even by his faction. The character of Locke, as a man of business, is painted with no other pencils than those of ridicule, and the diplomacy of Grotius and of Sir William Temple are utterly contemned; but their literary and philosophical works, the beauteous offspring of retirement and study, will continue to charm,

> " 'Till Time, like him of Gaza, in his wrath,
> Plucking the pillars that support the world,
> In nature's ample ruins lies entombed,
> And midnight, universal midnight, reigns."

Though in the text we are admonished to commune with ourselves in our chamber, yet it would be a very partial and narrow
interpretation if it were concluded that we could not meditate any-
where else. The secrecy of a closet and the stillness of midnight
are unquestionably propitious to the powers of reflection. But
other places and other seasons may be selected for that salutary
discipline which the Psalmist recommends. It is a vulgar error
to suppose that retirement and contemplation are never to be
found except in a forest or a desert, a cell or a cloister. In the
thronged mart, and in the blaze of day, he who has inured himself to habits of abstraction may commune with himself as though
he was in his chamber. Proofs of this abound in many a page
of the records of literature. Some of the fairest displays of self-
knowledge, some of the finest results of meditation, some of the
sweetest fruits of retirement owed their appearance not to the
tranquillity of sylvan groves. In many a metropolis, resounding
with the din of commerce and crowded with the throng of nations,
contemplation has had her fill. Though a sublime poet, in a fit
of rural enthusiasm, has exclaimed,
"Hide me from day's garish eye,"
yet it would be alike dangerous and delusive to believe that we
cannot speculate at noon as well as at night. In short, the choice
of time or place is not essential to the formation of habits of self-
sequestration and the acquisition of the precious power of withdrawing the mind from all external objects.

As, in Dr. Johnson's phrase, I am often wakefully disturbed
at midnight, and as I have not wholly forgotten my boyish attachment to woods and meadows, I acknowledge that I often
commune with myself in my chamber, and in genial seasons, by
the banks of a romantic river or in the recesses of a lonely forest.
I have already speculated twice on the profit and pleasure produci-
ble by nocturnal hours, wisely employed, and rural rambles, ju-
diciously directed. But for a period of no inconsiderable duration, I have often retired to rest at a vulgar hour, and have wholly
exchanged the country for the city. Change of circumstances demanded new habits. Though but seldom I wind slowly o'er the
lea; though the glimmering landscape but rarely fades before my

sight, and my ears generally listen to other sounds than the drowsy tinklings of a shepherd's bell, yet it is my duty to reflect much, even in the midst of confusion. Accordingly, I commune with my own heart in the crowd, and can be still, even in the street. I sermonize in the suburbs, and find apt alliteration in an alley. I start a topic in High Street, and hunt it down as far as Southwark or the Northern Liberties. I walk through the market place as I once wandered in a wood; and while one is talking of his farm, and another of his merchandize, I listen to the suggestions of fancy, or invoke the cherub contemplation.

But to return to a more rigorous exposition of the text, and consider it merely as an exhortation to the tranquil exercise of our mental powers in the retirement of the closet, I do not know whether in the pages of any philosopher I could find a better lesson of salutary discipline. It is favourable to the culture of intellectual, as well as moral habits. He who accustoms himself to closet meditations will not only purify his heart but correct his judgment, form his taste, exercise his memory, and regulate his imagination. Moreover, he then has an admirable opportunity to view the world at a due distance, to form a deliberate estimate of life, to calculate with precision the proportion of his own powers combined with those of other men; and having weighed himself, as it were, in the "balance of the sanctuary," to find new causes for regret and new reasons for reformation.

To multitudes, solitude, retirement, and reflection appear in a form more horrid than the weird sisters in Shakspeare. The man of business, the man of pleasure, the votary of vanity, and the victim of lassitude, all sedulously shun those hours which have been so nobly employed by philosophers, poets, hermits, and saints. Dr. Young, who has immortalized his self-communion in one of the most original poems in our language, a poem not only of gorgeous metaphors but of the most ardent piety, exclaims, with more than mortal enthusiasm,

> "Oh, lost to virtue, lost to manly thought,
> Lost to the noblest sallies of the soul!
> Who think it solitude to be alone.
> Communion sweet! communion large and high!
> Our reason, guardian angel, and our God!"

IV

On Prosperity and Adversity

"Also the Lord gave Job twice as much as he had before.
Then came there unto him all his brethren, and all his
sisters, and all they that had been of his acquaintance
before, and did eat bread with him in his house: and they
bemoaned him, and comforted him over all the evil that the
Lord had brought upon him: every man also gave him a
piece of money, and every one an ear-ring of gold.
—*Job* xiii. 10, 11.

Of all the dramatic poems with which readers of taste and sensibility have been delighted and instructed, the book of Job is unquestionably the most pathetic, sublime, and beautiful. The dialogue is in the noblest style of composition, and the interlocutors are all remarkable for character, manners, and sentiment. The fable is extremely artful and well supported, and the moral such as must challenge the approbation of every virtuous mind. He who is habitually negligent of his Bible or indifferent to the charms of the Oriental muse, will hardly be persuaded that the book of Job abounds with entertainment as well as instruction. But the fact is indisputable, and the politest scholars and the most rigorous critics have dwelt with rapture, which they felt, upon the beauties of this incomparable performance.

The personage whose name gives a title to the work is represented as an eastern nobleman of consummate wisdom, ardent piety, and unbounded wealth. He is neither insolent in prosperity nor abject in adversity. His character is emphatically described as perfect. Studious of the divine favour, and blind to all the blandishments of vice, he walked so uprightly in a noble and undeviating course of rectitude that he was universally regarded as the standard of integrity. He was perfectly pure from every taint of avarice, voluptuousness, hypocrisy, vanity, and ambition. He is neither ostentatious, envious, nor revengeful. His hospitality was princely, his justice exemplary, and his charities innumerable. He is a tender parent, a generous master, a constant friend, and a benevolent man. He was a father to the poor, the champion of the oppressed, the advocate of innocence, the guardian of orphans, and a physician to the lame and blind. In short, to use his own

[107]

brilliant and energetic expressions, he put on righteousness and it clothed him. His judgment was as a robe and a diadem. He caused the widow's heart to sing for joy, and the poor man was warmed with the fleece of his sheep.

But neither a prosperous fortune, nor a magnificent expenditure, nor a blameless life is a sure protection against the vicissitudes of nature, the ravages of disease, or the visitation of melancholy. While Job was thus basking in the meridian of happiness, while he enjoyed favour with God and popularity among men; while his palaces glittered with the gold of Ophir, the precious onyx, and the sapphire, coral and pearls, the ruddiest of rubies, and the topaz of Ethiopia, a terrible visitation is impending. The genius of misfortune appears before his distracted eyes in the most horrible form that fables yet have feigned, or fear conceived. In one hour his wealth vanished, his servants were slain, and his children consumed. To add to this gloomy catalogue of woes, his body is not only tormented with the scourge of sickness but his mind is clouded with all the darkness of despair.

In this mournful reverse of circumstances, one who took but a hasty glance at human nature and who partially looked only at one side would naturally conclude that Job would be immediately surrounded by crowds, impatient to testify their opinion of his value and their sorrow and solace for his suffering. As he was a man of genius, wisdom, and eloquence; as he had been a character of so much distinction that he was the companion of princes and the oracle of the people; as he was a nobleman, a judge, an orator, and a statesman, he had the strongest claim upon the gratitude of some, the friendship of others, and the compassion of all. Let us now count this army of auxilaries coming to the support of suffering virtue. We shall not laboriously task our arithmetic. Of that swarm which once buzzed in his courts and hovered in his palaces, who quaffed the richest of his wines and anointed themselves in rivers of his oil, only *three* individuals remain, and this scanty group, so far from pouring balm on his tortured mind, assail him in the angriest terms of reproach and controversy, and, in a spirit of captious sophistry which would disgrace the most illiberal of mankind, cavil at every chapter of his life. Instead of being run after by admiring thousands, instead of witnessing a multitude banqueting at his table, instead of being surrounded with obsequious guests and fawning dependents, he finds himself on a sudden in the dismal company of solitude and contempt. The same gust of adversity which had made a wreck of his fortune and his peace had blown away all his friends, connexions, and companions too, and on a raging ocean he finds himself joyless and alone, and on the very gulf of despair.

Like April skies, life is coquettish, capricious, and changeable. Prosperity and adversity often succeed each other, like the vicissitudes of day and night. The unhappy sufferer whom we have just left in an abyss of misfortunes, suddenly emerges, by the favour of Divine Providence, and his last days are fairer than the first. Having exercised a patience unparalleled and displayed a conscience void of offence, his integrity is justly and graciously requited by a most magnificent reward. His fortune was doubled, and his family favoured. Honours and gifts await him. But is it necessary for me to record, with the minuteness of an annalist, this second epoch in this good man's history? Is it not already indicated, as it were with a pen of diamond, by the circumstance in the text? Is it not clear as noontide beams that our patient hero must have gained his rank in society and become "a prosperous gentleman," before his brethren and his sisters and all they that had been of his acquaintance before, would come and eat bread with him and bemoan him and comfort him? During the gloomy season of his sufferings, we do not hear one syllable of these sunshine friends. Lover and friend were not put far away, but kept far away. No brother nor sister, nor old acquaintance, nor grateful friend, nor pampered guest, nor faithful servant, ever dreamed of visiting Job in poverty and affliction. Suddenly fortune smiles, and who then more smiling than the servile and parasitical followers of Fortune? The indigent Job is alone, the affluent Job is overwhelmed with the civilities of crowds. Not only his family friends and domestic retainers are officious in their visits, but every man gave him a piece of money, and every one an earring of gold. As Jaques in the play finely remarks,

> "They made a testament
> As worldlings do, giving their sum of more
> To that, which had too much."

There was a time, when Job sat down among the ashes, that, so far from receiving money gratuitously, he could not have borrowed a piece of silver, no, not on usury. But when his coffers and caskets are once more replenished, all the gold of the Orientals is showered upon him.

Having incidently alluded to a passage in the immortal Shakspeare, I cannot refrain from recommending to my classical readers the perusal, in connexion with my text, of that admirable drama, *Timon of Athens*. The story of this prodigal nobleman, compared with that of the patient Job deserted by his friends at his utmost need and courted by them during a reverse of fortune, will present such a picture of human nature as neither Hobbes nor Mandeville would hope to emulate with the hardest pencils and the darkest colouring.

V

Paul's Voyage to Rome

"Now, when much time was spent, and when sailing was now dangerous, Paul admonished them, and said unto them, 'Sirs, I perceive that this voyage will be with hurt and much damage, not only of the lading and ship, but also of our lives.' Nevertheless, the centurion believed the master and the owner of the ship, more than those things which were spoken by Paul."—*Acts* xvii. 7, 10, 11.

THIS affectionate admonition so modestly, so courteously, so benignantly expressed, claimed and deserved all the centurion's regard. But this appeal, both to the reason and the passions of a Roman soldier, was ineffectual. The warning voice of sagacity, the counsel of prudence, and even the silver tones of eloquence itself, neither convinced nor persuaded vulgar obstinacy. Why? Because "the centurion believed the master and the owner of the ship, more than those things which were spoken by Paul." The genius of fore-knowledge herself, personified by an apostle, rears her aspiring form on the Cretan strand and darts her eyes of keenness across the Adriatic gulf. She sees, in the gloomy distance, every image of night and tempest and terror; she sees the shattered mast and hears the howl of the tempest and the shrieks of the mariner. She exclaims in her most friendly voice to the centurion and his companions: "Beware, my Julius, beware my brethren, weigh not anchor; winter at Crete, unfurl no sail, till genial spring time come and south winds softly blow."

Is it possible that men will not listen to such a monitor? Is the deaf adder always an emblem of human perverseness, which will not hearken to the voice of the charmer, charming ever so wisely? Yes, it seems to be a characteristic of our nature often to treat with contemptuous neglect advice the most salutary, and prophesyings the most authentic, and to rush with desperate zeal, hoodwinked, to perdition.

But I shall not detain my readers with moralizing, which they may think dulness, when it is in my power to describe a voyage which I am sure they will pronounce entertaining.

To understand the full import of Paul's caution against the cen-

[111]

turion's carelessness, and the sinister consequences which followed from the latter, let us look into the last chapter of the Acts. It is short, but it is exceedingly copious of amusement and instruction.

In consequence of the zeal of St. Paul in defence of the Christian faith, he is accused, tried, and condemned before a provincial tribunal. He appeals, and is ordered to embark for Rome. This voyage to Italy commences with very evil omen. The accused apostle first enters into a ship of Adramyttium. But the winds are contrary. After being tossed about, and crossing two seas, the desired haven is still at a distance, and at Myra an Alexandrian vessel receives our illustrious wanderer. Here again, navigation is checked. Some torpedo seems to cling to the keel. The winds will not suffer the ship to pursue her course. They sailed slowly many days. Their lagging progress is finely described by almost every word in the context. The line labours almost as much as the ship. They could hardly pass one of the petty islands in the Mediterranean. They have not yet lost sight of Candia. Meanwhile, autumn advances. Much time has ben lost, and though the halcyon now sits brooding on the unruffled wave, yet winter and tempest and trouble are at hand. The deceitful tranquility of the sea and sky did not delude Paul. He needed no almanac to foretell him of the foul weather which approached, nor took an observation, except by the glass of experience and sagacity. He discerned mischief at the very verge of the horizon, in the little cloud no bigger than a man's hand. He told his fellow passengers plainly that the voyage would prove perilous, not merely to the vessel and cargo but to themselves. He doubtless enforced his admonition with all the arguments which his dexterous logic could so adroitly employ, and all that blandishment which his graceful elocution could lavish. In short, he appealed directly not only to their good sense, but to their interest and to their fears. If wisdom, authority, genius, learning, insinuating manners, and versatile talents were ever combined in one man, and all employed for the benefit of his fellow-men, it was on this occasion. Julius, the centurion in whose custody St. Paul is detained, had just witnessed the astonishing powers of the apostle in the course of his arduous trial before king Agrippa and the captious Festus, before a Jewish

viceroy and a Roman procurator, both of them his mortal enemies. On this interesting occasion, the apostle displayed so much
eloquence, assisted by all the powers of reason, innocence, truth,
and nature, that even his austerer judge, relenting, is almost won
over to Christianity, and both Agrippa and Festus, with a har-
mony that does them honour, agree that this fascinating man deserved neither death nor disgrace; that he might have been liberated
had he not appealed to a higher tribunal. The centurion was so
forcibly struck with the generous qualities of this great man's
mind that, though he held him as a prisoner, he treated him with
the utmost humanity, and on their arrival at Sidon, he had so
much confidence in his honour and integrity, and so much compassion for his misfortunes that, as it is beautifully expressed in
the original, Julius courteously entreated Paul, and gave him liberty to go unto his friends to refresh himself. Yet with all these
favourable impressions, this polite and gentle and generous soldier,
like too many men of the world, was swayed by ignorant, mechanical, and mercenary people, and trusted vulgar credulity rather
than philosophic genius. Although he had such recent experience
of the abilities of the apostle, nevertheless—I am ashamed to add
the miserable and disgraceful conclusion—nevertheless, the centurion believed the master and the owner of the ship more than those
things which were spoken by Paul. A venal owner of the cargo
and an ignorant mariner, who, as it appears, had scarcely a chart
to steer by, put to silence even the tongue of the apostle. Thus
does the "learned pate duck to the golden fool;" thus, in common
life, is the honourable merchant supplanted by the vulgar pedler,
thus is the scholar often defeated by the dunce, and thus does the
long-eared ass of drudgery sometimes gain more attention than the
fleetest zebra that ever bounded over the hills. The pilot and the
owner easily persuade the credulous centurion. The crew too, always restless and fond of change, are eager to depart. Because, in
their absurd opinion, the fair haven where they were at anchor in
safety was not perfectly commodious to winter in, "the more part
advised to depart thence, if by any means they might attain to
Phenice." These mad mariners consulted nothing but their own
impatient humour, listened to nothing but to that deceitful breeze

which is courted to waft them to some other port; and when the
south wind blew softly, supposing that they had obtained their
purpose, with all the credulity of foolishness and all the rashness
of desperation, they set sail, in defiance of Paul and of prudence
herself.

Let us mark the consequences of so romantic an adventure, instigated by the voice of the people and pursued by an opinionated
owner, a fool-hardy pilot, and a crew of madcap mariners who
probably, with all the plausibility of pert pretension, talked to the
good-natured centurion about tides and current as though inspired
by the very genius of the sea.

But not long after, there arose a tempestuous wind, called Euroclydon; and now we shall have a fine specimen of the skill of
these self-willed sailors. They are in the utmost confusion and
consternation. They abandon the vessel to the mercy of the
storm. She reels to and fro, with a motion more giddy than that
of the drunkards who have thus exposed her. The description is
so emphatical and picturesque in the original that it merits tran-
scription. "And when the ship was caught, and could not bear
up into the wind, we let her drive. And running under a certain
island, which is called Clauda, we had much work to come by the
boat, which, when they had taken up, they used helps, undergird-
ing the ship; and, fearing lest they should fall into the quicksands,
strake sail, and so were driven. And, we being exceedingly tossed
with the tempest, the next day they lightened the ship, and the
third day we cast out with our own hands the tackling. And
when *neither sun nor stars in many days appeared.* and no *small
tempest* lay on us, *all hope that we should be saved was then taken
away.*"

Virgil's description of a storm in the first book of an epic poem
which is the boast of ages and the darling of criticism, may be
more elaborate, yet is not more affecting than the above narrative.

But the misfortunes of these miserable mariners are by no means
at an end. During the space of a fortnight, a most tremendous
interval, the storm rages with unmitigated wrath. They are buf-
feted by all the billows of the Adriatic sea. At starless midnight,
dreading the peril of hidden rocks, they cast four anchors out of

the ship and wished for the day. Infatuated, intimidated men, how often did ye wish not only for the dawn of a serene morning, but that ye had listened to the voice of the saint and the sage, and not have loosed from Crete to have gained this harm and loss!

Though Paul had been so maltreated by these misguided men, he does not attempt to revenge himself in the height of their calamity. After calmly expostulating with them on the enormous absurdity of their conduct, his very next accents are those of comfort and consolation. He exhorts the dejected mariners to be of good cheer, and assures them that no life shall be lost; predicts, as from the beginning, the shipwreck as a punishment for their temerity, then renews his topics of cheerfulness and apprizes them that they will reach the island of Malta in safety.

Thus terminates the voyage of this crazy Alexandrian skiff, whose owner was self-love, whose helmsman was rashness, and whose sailors were blindness, caprice, and obstinacy. As might be expected, even by an individual of far less penetration than Paul, this ill-managed and ill-fated vessel ran aground, and a pitiful figure she makes on the shore, with her head stuck in the sand and her stern broken with the violence of the waves. The cargo gluts the sea, the ship is wrecked on the strand, and on disjointed planks and broken boards, overwhelmed with fear, harassed by hunger, drenched with rain, and benumbed with cold, instead of a secure haven and a comfortable home under the clement skies of their regretted Italy, the mariners find themselves on a barren rock and among a barbarous people.

Shakspeare, somewhere, describing a herd of a similar character to the crew in the text, remarks that "they'll take suggestion as a cat laps milk." Our rash mariners had all this facility. Without making a wry face they swallowed every word of the owner and master of the ship with as much ease as they would a sugared medicine, but it proved to be the bitterest pill they had ever taken, and as we have seen, aggravated all the horrors of their sea sickness to a tenfold degree.

We have now finished a narrative of this sinister voyage, which, we are afraid, as far as our own pen has been employed, will prove as fatiguing to our readers as it was to the remonstrating saint and

[115]

the rebellious crew. One natural inference shall now be drawn, which may be considered as the moral of this essay.

In every country, in every age, how often has this despicable farce of human perverseness been exhibited! How obstinately do men shut their eyes against the radiance of reason, and stop their ears to exclude the voice of truth!

In seasons of political peril, for example, how often has a sagacious statesman, whose wisdom and prescience have been tried, as it were, in a balance and uniformly stood the test of an unerring standard, cautioned in vain both the officer and the mariner not to embark madly in the crazy ship, Desperation. Some narrow calculation, some short-sighted policy, some giddy humour has predominated over experience, prudence, and genius. Men rush to their ruin. The Euroclydon rises. The bleak northeast of adversity howls in every ear. The fatal levanter sweeps the sea and the sky. The "fountains of the great deep are broken up," and our bark and the crew are dashed on the quicksands of destruction.

VI

Story of Samuel

"Moreover his mother made him a little coat, and brought
it to him from year to year."—*I Sam.* xi. 19.

IN the initial book of the kings of Israel, which, as it records
in a very noble style some of the most memorable events in Jewish
history, deserves the profoundest attention, perhaps there is nothing more pleasing and instructive than the biography of the
prophet Samuel. A circumstance, apparently trivial, which oc-
curred in his infancy, will form the subject of our present speculation.

We deliberately adopt the phrase "apparently trivial," because
the circumstance in question, though it might not be noticed by
the quick glance of hasty observation, led to the most important
results and contributed to the formation of one of the most splendid characters ever portrayed by the historian.

Descended from respectable ancestors from Mount Ephraim,
his father, who appears to be a tender husband, an affectionate
parent, and a truly religious man, was in the habit, as might be
naturally expected from so exemplary a character, of migrating
annually from the solitude of Mount Ephraim to the city of Shiloh. But the journey was not undertaken from the ordinary motives of curiosity, restlessness, indolence, or pleasure. He did not
forsake his rural retreat to gaze at the magnificence of a metropolis, or to hearken to the "hum of men." No: the object of the
journey was of a more noble nature, and worthy of the pious pil-
prim. He went up out of the city yearly to worship and to sacrifice in Shiloh, and to adore, in the Jewish temple, the Great Parent of the Universe.

Nor was his devotion of the sullen and monastic kind. There
was nothing selfish, melancholy, or austere in his religious service.
His family accompanied him and kneeled at the same altar. Hannah, his beloved consort, was so struck with the solemnity of the
temple and the beauty of holiness, her heart was so softened by the

[117]

spirit of piety, and her head so convinced of the propriety of her plan that, in an hour of melancholy yet sober enthusiasm, she resolved to dedicate her first born son to the church. In the simplicity of the Hebrew idiom, she *vowed a vow* that she would give him to the Lord all the days of his life. This good resolution did not evaporate in the idle words of a fanatic visionary. It was not the mere babble of a superstitious crone who mistakes the heat of the heart and the giddiness of the head for the emotions of rational zeal. The determination to dedicate her son to the priesthood was worthy of a discreet and amiable woman who probably saw, with the keen eyes of sagacity, assisted by the light of prescience, that Samuel would prove a personage eminent for his rank and piety, that he would dictate the operations of a campaign and preside at the deliberations of a cabinet, that he would predict the fate of empires and assist at the coronation of kings, that his warning voice would restrain the madness of the people and his pious orisons ascend to the heaven of his God.

All this was gloriously accomplished. While yet a child, he was distinguished by the particular partiality of Providence. He was endowed with the gift of prophecy and invested with the robes of religion. Though devoted to the service of God, he acquired popularity among men. During an important era in his life he was judge of south and west Israel, and afterwards of the other quarters. This viceroyalty included a power nearly absolute. With the voice potential of sovereign authority, he could exclaim unto the north, "Give up," and to the south, "Keep not back; bring thy sons from afar, and thy daughters from the ends of the earth." He was scarcely weaned, before we find him ministering in the Jewish tabernacle and superseding in religious ceremonies and offices the elder priesthood. In the maturity of manhood he administers justice, guards the purity of the national worship, and promotes the peace and dignity of government. He concludes famous treaties. He erects magnificent altars. Such was the splendour of his reputation and such the opinion of his discernment that the stranger Benjamite, who lived in remote obscurity, far from the scene of Samuel's glories, describes him as an honourable man, and adds, what every page in Samuel's history

proves, that *all that he saith cometh to pass*. He is saluted with
the sacred title of seer, and even the ungovernable populace, awed
by his abilities and sanctity, will not eat in the high place of the
city until he bless the sacrifice. He pours the oil of honour and
gladness on the head of a sovereign, and then, with all the skill of
a statesman and all the power of a premier, dictates the course of
regal polity. Though almost perpetually conversant with courts,
he is pure from their corruption. He is a faithful servant to his
prince, but he is also a vigilant guardian and an honest monitor.
While others flatter, he rebukes Saul; and although his sovereign
was of a moody, sullen, and untractable spirit, yet Samuel never
shrinks when it was necessary to adopt either the ardour of expostulation or the acerbity of censure. Though he thought as a
sage when he reflected upon the vices and follies of this monarch,
yet he felt like a man when he deplored their consquences. Obliged
to estrange himself from his infatuated sovereign, he still cherished
a sort of paternal solicitude for his welfare; and when the gloomy
king, in a fit of capricious disgust, went up to his house, and the
prophet came no more to see him until the day of his death, nevertheless, as it is expressed with equal artlessness and affection in the
sacred history, nevertheless Samuel mourned for Saul. In the decline of life, when most men, satiated with worldly grandeur,
slide carelessly down the slippery descent of age, this consistent and
illustrious character is erect and guarded to the last. Conscious of
his spotless integrity and of his fervid zeal in the public service,
he challenges a justification of his integrity in one of the noblest,
most rhetorical and pathetic passages that can be found in the
pleadings of any orator in any age. He said unto all Israel, "Behold I have hearkened unto your voice and have made a king over
you. And now behold the king walketh before you; and I am
old and gray-headed, and behold my sons are with you; and I
have walked before you from my childhood unto this day. Behold here I am; witness against me before the Lord, and before
his anointed: whose ox have I taken? or whose ass have I stolen?
or whom have I defrauded? Whom have I oppressed, or of whose
hand have I received any bribe to blind mine eyes therewith?
And I will restore it you." And they said "Thou hast not de-

frauded us, nor oppressed us, neither hast thou taken aught of any man's hand." "The Lord is witness against you, and his anointed is witness, that ye have not found aught in my hand." And they answered, "He is witness."

This is the *finis coronat opus;* this is leaving life's bustling scene with such excellent companions as honour, spirit, and dignity. The circumstances of this transaction give it a peculiar effect. It was a *provoco ad populum.* It was an appeal to the populace, to the mutable, miscellaneous, ungrateful, and ignorant rabble. It was, moreover, not only to a mob, but to a Jewish mob, than which the herd of swine of whom the devil himself once had the absolute possession does not exhibit a stronger picture of baseness, wildness, perverseness, and desperation. But even before so rash and stupid a tribunal, the manly voice of innocence, with dignity and integrity in her train, commanded silence and won applause; and what renders more signal this triumph of genius, virtue, and rank, is that it was obtained at the very moment when the intrepid prophet and indignant sage was reproving the herd for their ingratitude, obstinacy, and rebellion.

Having thus abridged the history of this great and good man as concisely as the nature and multitude of his illustrious actions would allow, we will now look back to the text, from which the vulgar critic may think we have strayed, but which the reader of sensibility will soon perceive has always been the radiant point of our speculation.

One eventful year in the life of Elkanah, the father of Samuel, he and all his house went up to offer the yearly sacrifice and his vow. But on this occasion one of the dearest of his domestic companions did not accompany the annual pilgrim in his journey to sacred Shiloh. *Hannah went not up.* This did not arise from female caprice or any decay of devotion. Her reason was a valid one; for she said unto her husband, I will not go up until the child be weaned, and then I will bring him, that he may abide there for ever. The favourite object of this tender mother was to give her son an excellent education, to instil into his mind all high, holy, and honourable principles, and to lead him to the fountains of wisdom. When the child was young, she took it up with her to the temple, and after presenting her gifts, according to the oriental custom, and making sacrifice, she remarked to the venerable high priest that for this child she had prayed; that her maternal wish was answered; and that as Heaven had granted her petition, to the service of Heaven this son should be devoted. He accordingly actually officiates at the altar, being a child girded with a linen ephod. Here some dissipated or mercenary mothers would have left him to take his chance, either to live by the altar like a priest, or to perish like one of its miserable victims. But the matron whom we now commemorate had not only a tender heart but a liberal spirit, a steady judgment, a perspicacious discernment, and that generous prudence which is the queen regent of all the virtues. She knew that youth, innocence, and inexperience ought to be assisted in their struggle through the thorns and brakes of the wilderness of this world. She was not satisfied with a single burst of maternal affection or with bounding her benignity by lines of distance or a term of years. She was fully apprized that a youth, engrossed by contemplation and study, would either have no leisure for domestic cares, or that in the abstraction of literature he would wholly lose sight of them; that hence he would be sometimes the natural prey of fraud and sometimes the victim of penury; and that the learning of the east would not procure him from strangers, either the linen ephod of the child or the mantle of the man. She was determined, therefore, habitually to take care that neither his mind, his health, nor his studies should sustain any detriment from the rude collision of petty cares. But as he was of a sober and studious humour, that the tranquillity of his hermit cell should never be violated, and that he should enjoy uninterrupted leisure to acquire that fund of information and those useful habits which might ultimately redound to his own honour and the general good. In accomplishing so judicious a design, she employed no agent but her own heart, and no deputy but her own skill.

The importance of such a provision has been abundantly verified in the history of Samuel's successful career. Had he been left solitary at Shiloh, neglected by his friends, exposed to the artifice of some and the temptation of others, he never would have prophesied any thing but his own ruin; and instead of being a judge, would in all probability have been a prisoner.

Wise and benignant mother! With how much enthusiasm and sensibility wilt thou always be apostrophized by every son, in every age, who has felt the fostering warmth of maternal affection!

In addition to thy acts of kindness, from the dawn of genius to its glorious meridian, thy periodical assiduity of attention shall be ever remembered! That little vestment which, to render the present more valuable, was brought, not by one of thine handmaids, not by a careless or venal slave, but by thy gracious self, will outlast the weaving of the noblest looms. Like the regretted handkerchief of the fabled Moor, in the unequalled tragedy of the matchless dramatist, "the worms were *hallowed* that did breed its silk." It made her son amiable, and there was magic in its web. But if the little coat made by a mother was not, as a poet's fancy might suggest, of a silken texture, it was of wool from a Gideon's fleece, and watered with the kindliest dews of Heaven.

VII

Story of Moses

"And he sat down by a well. Now the priest of Midian
had seven daughters: and they came and drew water, and
filled the troughs to water their father's flock. And the
shepherds came and drove them away: but Moses stood
up, and helped them, and watered their flock."
—*Exodus* xi. 15, 16, 17.

IN the juvenile days of Moses, that prophet, having unfortunately interfered in a quarrel between an Egyptian and a Jew, went
into voluntary exile. Provoked at the assassination of a subject,
the reigning monarch sought to slay Moses, who fled from his
wrath into the land of Midian. Here he took up his residence in
the vicinity of a well and led a sort of hermit's life, "unknowing
and unknown." By a glance at the history of pastoral ages, it
will be seen that the task of drawing water, either for household
purposes, or for the use of the fold, generally devolved upon wom-
en. The simplicity, the indolence, or the rudeness of the patriarchs caused them to forget that the obvious destination of the
softer sex was for lighter labour; and that men, as the natural
guardians of females, should ever rescue their fair wards from ignominious thraldom. But the priest of Midian, with all his learning, was, it seems, clownish and inattentive in this respect, for he
suffers his whole family of girls to "draw water, and fill the
troughs to water his flock." In those days, and in that arid region, reservoirs, wells, and cisterns attracted almost as great crowds
as fashionable watering places have in times more modern, and in
a climate less fiery. Indeed, throughout the east, wells were a
kind of haunt; and at their margin were to be found pilgrims and
patriarchs, shepherds and herdsmen, blushing beauties and clamorous boors, all eager to allay their own thirst or that of the animals
lowing and bleating around. In such a promiscuous crowd,
grossness and incivility would always mingle, perhaps predominate; and not only delicate ears but even graceful forms would
sometimes be wounded. The daughters of the Egyptian priest
did not repair to the well of Midian without exposure to the at-

tacks of brutality. Certain shepherds of the country, "fellows of the baser sort," in all probability Midianitish *democrats,* influenced by the wonted churlishness, impudence, boorishnes, and ferocity of the republican character, came and drove these unoffending females away. Perceiving this harshness and, in a spirit of gallantry, resenting it, Moses, with the courtesy of a cavalier, quitted his seat and his meditations, civilly helped the insulted maidens, and relieved them from the labour of watering their flocks. This is a pleasing instance of primeval politeness, and demonstrates that even in the simplest stages of society, the man of feeling, taste, and judgment, will always support the rights of woman.

The sex have a paramount claim to our protection, tenderness, and courtesy. Years cannot cause my dim eyes to survey the fair carelessly, or with indifference. My heart still palpitates at their approach, and in despite of the discipline of philosophy, my nerves vibrate like the keys of a harpsicord, from the lightest touch of a charmer. Once, in the absurd misapprehension of youth, I thought the character of a woman-hater worth imitating, and even attempted to hurl a feeble lance at the daughters of Eve. But time has taught me the impolicy and baseness of such a warfare. I have not only made a truce, but concluded a firm and lasting peace with the ladies. I pride myself that they still admit an old bachelor to their toilets, and that they will not refuse a dropped fan, though presented to them by a gray-headed gallant. If I hear the pleasing rustle of silk against my study stairs, I make shift to hide my spectacles, and at the expense of my gouty limbs, cheerfully resign my obsolete arm chair to the occupancy of the fair sex. I am a very Moses to resent any ill treatment they may receive; and did modern ladies watch and water sheep, like the seven shepherdesses of Midian, I am sure I should "right merrily" fill the bucket.

The gallantry of the attentive Moses was not unrequited. It procured him an invitation to the house of the priest whose daughters had been thus protected by the shield of civility. The fruits of good breeding were the gratitude of a venerable divine, and the hand of Zipporah his daughter.

Thus it may be learned by every young man eager for a pleasant

passage through life, that attention to women honours both the
giver and the receiver. Nothing is to be gained by rudeness to the
sex. By complaisance to them, much may be acquired. He who
is universally decried by women is rarely very poular in male society. Nature intended the two sexes should live in amity. Let the
good understanding continue. If we treat our female friends with
courtesy and with tenderness, if we listen to their voice with attention, bow at their approach, and sigh at their departure, we
shall be liberally remunerated. Selfishness alone will dictate such
politeness. Woman, naturally frank, generous, and sensitive, will
hasten to discharge the obligation. On him who is thus watchful
to please her she will smile with radiance, she will smooth his pillow, she will, like Hotspur's consort, "sing the song that pleases
him," and "bind his aching head with flowers."

VIII

The Man of Understanding

"When thou seest a man of understanding, get thee betimes unto him, and let thy feet wear the steps of his door."—*Ecc.* vi. 36.

YES, in a world of weak ones it is our duty, it will be our pleasure, and, ye selfish generation, it will be for our interest too, to yield favours to the wise and bread to men of understanding. Our patronage will be but rarely exercised, and few will be the loaves for these wise men to devour, for I looked, and lo! they are a solitary and scanty band, unobtrusive, like the hermit of the mountains.

But though the "man of undertsanding" is rarely to be seen, and though it would profit us much under the sun to gather the honey of his lips, such is our perverseness, our folly, or our fate, that, untrodden by our feet, we suffer the moss to gather on the "steps of his door."

My study window overlooks the house of an eminent physician. He understands accurately the nice movements of the human machine; he is a botanist, skilled in the properties of plants, the cedar of Libanus, and the "hyssop on the wall;" he has meditated on the system of nature, and he has tried many of the processes of art. I see him turning over the volumes which contain the secrets of medicine, and I hear him describe skilfully the various modes to blunt or to extract the arrows of disease. But alas! my careless countrymen, "all this availeth him nothing." The blind, the maim, and the halt of our villages refuse bread to this "man of understanding" and measure their wheat in brimming bushels to the quack who cannot distinguish between a fever and the gout, who applies his nippers to a wart and thinks he extracts a cancer, who poisons you with antimony, curdles your blood with calomel, drenches you with enfeebling teas, and, as a wit once expressed it, prescribes draughts so neutral, they declare neither for the patient nor the malady. If the Royal Preacher in whose writings I find my text had seen whole villages clamorous, at the midnight hour, for a fetid quack and his powders, and "passing by on the other side" when they see the regular practitioner, he would have forgotten for a moment all the wisdom of the East and, like provoked Peter in the Gospel, would "curse and swear" at such egregious folly.

Those of my readers who will gladly turn out of the paths of error when they hear a warning voice behind them, "Here is a better path; walk therein," will, I hope, learn the value of "men of understanding." When their value is once known, the "steps of their door" will be hourly ascended. They will teach us how to think, to speak, and to act. If divines, they will not attempt to persuade you that Heaven cannot be taken but by the violence of Scotch divinity. If lawyers, they will not demand exorbitant fees to support a rotten cause. If physicians, you will hear them utter no words more cramp than "temperance" and "regimen." If moralists, they will mark the difference between wisdom and cunning, they will point out the weakness, as well as wickedness, of those petty frauds, those iniquitous contracts, those trickling arts of jockeyship, so frequent and so disgraceful among a rural people, where nought but simplicity should be found. To such divines you will cheerfully vote the amplest salary, and you will receive in exchange that wisdom which, we are assured in a volume of the highest authority, is better than rubies.

IX

On Versatility

"For though I be free from all men, yet have I made
myself servant to all, that I might gain the more. To the
weak, became I as weak, that I might gain the weak:
I am made all things to all men."—*I Cor.* ix. 19, 22.

IN this description of pliability, St. Paul exhibits a happy likeness of his own character, and justifies by his own illustrious and
moral example the excellency of an accommodating spirit. There
is scarcely any feature in the characters of mankind that I view
with more complacency than that useful and pleasing versatility
for which so many "shining ones" have been conspicuous, and
which has so liberally contributed to social gratification. As we
are, in the holy writings, shadowed out under the picturesque
image of "strangers and pilgrims," merely visiting or wandering
in this world, it behoves us so to fashion our deportment that,
whether we call at the palace, the caravansary, or the cottage, we
may conform to the habits of the respective proprietor. When
discoursing on the utility of this mode of pleasing, it will not be
suspected that I advocate shameful and vicious compliances. My
uniform tone of preaching denies this, and every candid reader
will draw with me the line of demarcation between the social and
salutary doctrine of the saint of Tarsus, and the selfish and hypocritical sycophancy begotten at St. Omer's, and bred in the house
of Stanhope.

Plutarch, a writer eminent for morality, has left us the character
of Alcibiades, that real Proteus of the ancients, and from the fondness with which that pleasing biographer insists upon the varied
habits and manners of his hero, it is evident that much of the versatility of the accommodating Athenian is proposed as a model
to imitate, not as an example to deter. The vice of the son of
Clinias is abundantly reproved by Plutarch, but he proves, in the
course of a narration of the most artless simplicity, that in much
of the storm and conflict of life, the yielding willow is to be
preferred to the resisting oak. By his pliancy, Alcibiades not only

[128]

could "charm the mistress, and fix the friend," but could adorn the senate and extend empire. To this spirit the Athenians were more than once indebted for political pre-eminence and safety; and no higher praise of his flexibility can be sought than that Socrates was his tutor and friend. Half a page of Plutarch gives a bright portrait of this courtier, and it will be useful earnestly to gaze at an object so dazzling. Among the Spartans, he forgot the delicacy of Athenian tables. He was austere in his habits, indefatigable in exercise, sparing of speech. In Asia, he talked in the florid style of mirth, and pleasure, and luxury, and ease. In Thrace, devoted to horsemanship and brimming cups, he rode like a jockey and drank like a fox-hunter. In the palace of a Persian grandee, the pliant form of the courtly stranger was invested with flowing purple; and among a magnificent people he discoursed of the "gorgeous east," and of "royal state," and of the "wealth of Ormus and of Ind," and, like prince Bonbobbin, in the fairy tales, nothing fell from his mouth but gems and gold.

Another brilliant example of this happy and complying temper is to be found in the character of Charles Townsend, one of the chancellors of the exchequer of England, than whom, the younger Lyttelton excepted, a more dazzling meteor never flashed within the walls of St. Stephen's Chapel. He was a wit, a courtier, a man of business, at will. He could, like Bolingbroke, harangue, "seduce and impose" in the senate. He was a Yorick at the table, a Chesterfield at the toilet, a Fox at the tavern, and a Pitt at the desk. Burke describes him as a "luminary;" and nothwithstanding the orator of Beaconsfield, in the heat of political controversy, is inveighing against him as a statesman of principles opposite to his own and, in his opinion, ruinous to his country, yet he talks of him as a "prodigy," and as the best reason for his popularity, adds that "he conformed exactly to the temper of the house of commons, and seemed to guide, because he was always sure to follow it." He every day adapted himself to the disposition of others and adjusted himself before it, as at a looking-glass; he was the delight and ornament of parliament and the charm of every private society. To please universally was the object of his life. He was always in perfect unison with his associates; and, as a climax to this most flattering description of an illustrious character, Mr. Burke adds that he had no failings which were not owing to a noble cause, to an ardent, generous passion for fame, a passion which is the instinct of all great souls. No man can read this vivid detail of the charms of versatility without acknowledging its mighty operation in adorning and smoothing life; and as it is our duty to enlarge the fund of social pleasure, let it be impressed on every youthful mind that the bending humour of Townsend is more pleasant, and more profitable too, than the austere rigidity of John Knox, or the proud obstinacy of the Earl of Chatham.

Dean Swift, whose aversion to courtiers was notorious, and who, from the sullen misanthropy of his character, may be justly called an impartial witness, has borne the most honourable testimony in favour of the talents described in our text. Among the favourites of that writer was Charles Mordaunt, Earl of Peterborough, a nobleman no less signalized for his gallantry in Queen Ann's wars than for his skill in pleasing, his variety of talents, and the high power of varying his means to attain more effectually the end. In a short copy of verses which, far from being merely complimentary, contain a faithful description of the universal talents of the hero of Barcelona, the Dean of St. Patrick's, after observing in the initial lines of his poem, that

> "Mordanto fills the trump of fame,
> And prints are crowded with his name,"

proceeds to give such a lively sketch of versatility itself that my readers will easily indulge my usual habit of quotation:

> "In journeys he outstrides the post,
> Sits up till midnight with his host,
> Talks politics, and gives the toast.
> Shines in all climates like a star;
> In senates bold, and fierce in war;
> A land commander, and a tar."

Examples and topics to support the theory and practice of St. Paul crowd upon me, and the usual portion of paper assigned me by my printer already overflows with my swelling sermon. The subject will be resumed and finished in my next speculation. Meanwhile, let my readers be satisfied with a profile of the versatile powers, and wait till "a more convenient season," for a full-length picture.

X

On Versatility

"For though I be free from all men, yet have I made
myself servant unto all, that I might gain the more. To
the weak became I as weak, that I might gain the weak:
I am made all things to all men."—*I Cor.* ix. 19, 22.

RESTRICTED by the narowness of my page, and opulent in
the variety of my topics, I could only, in my last sermon, accomplish half my purpose. Those of my patient readers who are willing to follow me pursuing one subject for a fortnight, may find
my design completed in the following speculation.

Without much attention to chronological order, a few examples
of the pleasures and uses flowing from versatility have been already cited. It would have been more methodical to have illustrated the subject by an early description of the character of that
amiable apostle whose conduct was the brightest commentary
upon the doctrine so perspicuously detailed in my text. It is not
too late to be accurate, and to be just; and on the short strip of paper that is allowed me, I will strive to combine such particulars
of the pupil of Gamaliel as will exemplify and strengthen my subject.

Among the earlier assertors of the dignity and purity of the
Christian faith, none equalled St. Paul in combining, with the
most erect piety, the most pliant politeness. His courtesy and his
Christianity went hand in hand; and during the infancy of a per-
secuted sect, harassed by the intolerance of paganism and the tyr-
anny of provincial governors, the gentleness of his demeanor was
the surest mode to render his doctrine palatable to the frowning
Roman, the supercilious Jew, and the fastidious Greek. A religious reformer, at a moment so unpropitious to innovation, would
have retarded the cause dearest to his heart if it could be said of
him, as of the hypocritical deputy in Shakspeare,

"Lord Angelo is precise,
Stands as a guard with envy, scarce confesses
That his blood flows, or that his appetite
Is more to bread than stone."

[131]

Had Paul been thus rigid, he would have half strangled Christianity in its cradle, and an earlier martyrdom would have attested the
weak judgment of the saint.   He was too much a man of the
world to affect such austerity.   With a generous frankness he
avows his frailty, his "weakness and wanderings."   "We also are
men of like passions with you," is his honest language; and
whether we find him with pharisees or sadducees, in the Areopagus of Athens or before the judgment seat of Agrippa, he is equally the courtier, willing to comply with the modes of fashion, willing to yield to trivial prejudices for the sake of reconciling obstinacy and incredulity to his momentous schemes.   At Thessalonica,
in a Jewish synagogue, he reasoned from scripture premises in so
candid and polite a manner that many, even of that bigoted nation, consorted with Paul, and none but "the baser sort," as they
are emphatically called—men upon whom the smiles of civility
beam in vain—none but those "lewd" and despicably low "fellows," rejected his salutary proffers.   At Berea, both men and
ladies of quality were allured to the Christian scheme, no less by
the address of the apostle than by a conviction of the truths he
preached.   Even in the market-place at Athens, among philosophers and other rabble, such was the adroitness of this polished
denizen of Tarsus that some, even of the superficial, sceptical, and
volatile Athenians, were willing to "hear again" when he urged
the mysterious doctrine of the resurrection of the dead.   At Corinth, we read that he "persuaded both Jews and Greeks."   To effect this, strikingly exemplifies the flexibility of his temper and the
variety of his talents; he must have possessed both the recondite
lore of the first and the tongues of the second, to have conciliated
such intractable characters.   His valedictory oration to the elders
of Ephesus is a perfect model of the polite style; by his bland and
insinuating accents he twice softened the ruggedness of soldiers
and procured some remission of the punishment arbitarily inflicted
by biassed or corrupt tribunals.   When the saint perceived that the
ecclesiastical court of Ananias was torn into schism by the sectaries
of the day, by artfully applying to the prejudices of the sadducees
and the pharisees, and exciting a controversy among them respecting the verity of their peculiar tenets, he escaped persecution for the

time and obtained an appeal to Felix, at Cesarea. His reply to the abuse of the loquacious Tertullus is insinuating, mild, and courtly, and so captivated the corrupt Felix that this prejudiced governor suffered him to have free access to his friends and to enjoy some mitigation of his confinement. The exordium of his elegant plea before Agrippa has been frequently cited as a brilliant example of the most artful application to the vanity and prejudices of a stern judge that was ever employed in a court of justice. The effect was magical and vindicates the power of versatility. Bigotry relented, Persecution dropt his sanguinary scourge; and Truth and Mercy, through the organs even of this partial tribunal, proclaimed loudly, saying, "This man doeth nothing worthy of death or bonds."

In whatever situation we contemplate this shining saint, we find him ever pliant, polite, persuasive, and of the hue of his companions. At Sidon he attracts the favours of the courteous Julius. On shipboard, and tossed by the lawless surges of the Adriatic, he softens the boisterous mariner. In Rome, by doing what the Romans did, he dwells in his own house two years peaceably. His language is that of bland civility. He uses the winning phrase "fellow-soldier" and "fellow-labourer." He has no narrow rule of sociability. He consorts indifferently with Luke the physician and Zenas the lawyer, and talks in the festal tone of Gaius, mine host. He is glad that Stephanas and Fortunatus are come, and seems to regret that Demas should go. His politeness is universal. He commends "Phebe our sister," and greets Mary and Julia. Whether it is "the beloved Persis," or Tryphena and Tryphosa, 'tis all one to the saint! he can salute both or either. Such a character must be loved. Such gentleness has the general suffrage.

> "Him, portion'd maids, apprenticed orphans blest,
> The young who labour, and the old who rest."

In the early part of my life, while I was mingling with men, and oftener in the city than in my closet, I was acquainted and charmed with an European gentleman whose versatility, universal knowledge, and fascinating powers, almost persuaded me that he was a magician, or the wandering Jew himself. As this extraordinary and agreeable acquaintance afforded a lively proof of the advantages of an accommodating temper, I beg permission to sketch, in my rude way, one more picture, and I can affirm it is done from a masterly original.

I believe it is Dr. Smollet, who, in one of his novels, describes the hero in company with a grave, plodding citizen. Adapting himself to the humour of his entertainer, the pliable guest smokes tobacco though he was averse to the plant, derides idlers, talks of cent. per cent. and harangues upon the funds like a professed broker. My European acquaintance acted in the very spirit of this species of facility. Like the Aristippus of the Roman poet, every hue of life became him. He seemed to realize the Ovidian fable of incessant metamorphosis, and classical enthusiasm might fancy him the ever-varying Proteus, recent from his coral cave. He was, at pleasure, a poet, a painter, a musician, a divine. With men of learning and wit, he poured forth the copious stores of extensive erudition. With ladies, he discussed the pretensions of rival coquettes, or described the tints of a modish ribband. In the joviality of wine, his chorus was in unison with vociferating revellers, and by the couch of the invalid, or at the toilet of beauty, his voice was modulated to the lowest and sweetest tones. I have seen him with a musician, and he held a harp in his hand and played enchantingly a favourite air and spoke scientifically of the theory of harmonics. I have seen him with poets, and he talked for hours, with critical precision, of a disputed passage in Virgil or Shakspeare. Three fat-headed American speculators, calling upon him one evening, he interested all their avarice by proposing a thousand projects of plausible adventure. I have heard him talk on subjects of commerce with a merchant, and he spoke of debentures and cockets, and clearance, like a custom-house officer. Among the clergy, who so well read as he in St. Basil and church history? Among lawyers he took care to remember anecdotes of sergeant Singleton, and Lord Mansfield, and to quote, with technical propriety, the pleadings of the one and the decisions of the other. In fine, he was a general actor. But whatever was his cast of parts, he could play them well. He was the Garrick of life and his delighted audience gave him all their applause.

XI

Story of Samson

"Then went Samson to Gaza, and saw there an
harlot."—*Judges* xvi. i.

STRONG as he was, such a journey debilitated him. It was not
the length of the way from Timnath; it was not the rugged road
nor the irksomeness of a hard-trotting mule; it was not a stroke
of the sun nor a bleak air that shook the nerves and prostrated
the life of Samson, for not one of these circumstances is even
glanced at by the historian; no, he saw in one of the stews of
Gaza a venal beauty, and was undone. His wit evaporated, his
wisdom turned babbler, he lost his vigilance, his eyes, and his life.

One licentious indulgence excites to another. The blandishments of this courtezan allure to the cells of the whole sisterhood.
He lays his head in the lap of voluptuousness and gives full scope
to criminal desire. For it came to pass, afterward, that he loved a
woman in the valley of Sorek, whose name was Delilah.

Let us ponder a little the history of these unlucky amours. A
sketch of the wars and vicissitude of passion is of more interest
than the narrative of a battle or siege or the annals of empire.

To display a striking, as well as useful contrast, it may be correct to view Samson before he entered the gates of Gaza, and
after his acquaintance with two bad women.

His first was by no means a love adventure. It was in the style
of chivalry, without a damsel. Lurking in the vines of a rude
territory, a lion roared against our juvenile hero who, as it is in a
lively manner expressed, rent his ferocious adversary as he would
have rent a kid. A bold encounter, but not half so dangerous as
the smiles of the lady in the valley of Sorek. Mere brute force,
however, was not the sole attribute of Samson. For seven days
he tortures the ingenuity of thirty friends to resolve an enigma.
He has the palm of wit and the chaplets of victory; by his art he
destroys the property, and by his arm the life of his enemies. Not
only the family of his father, Manoah, but the whole circumjacent

region must have rung with the praises of this youth of promise; and even indifferent men and abstract reasoners would alertly from such imposing premises draw the happiest conclusion.

But behold how, in one hour, so great riches come to nought. Thus far, what a tissue of brilliant achievements do we admire. The next scene is madly mortifying. In the very summary of the ensuing page of his story, what are the humiliating particulars of his downfall? Samson, the valiant, the witty, and the wise, is the dupe of female jugglers; is enticed, is overcome. In the arms of a "twining Lais" of the Philistines, his supernatural strength melts away. He awakes out of this lethargy of pleasure and hopes to go out, as at other times, rejoicing in his might. But the energy of his soul is no more. He whom once nothing could restrain, is bound. He grinds in the prison house, and dwindled into a buffoon, is invested with his motley to amuse the rabble.

In the life of this extraordinary personage it is matter of regretful speculation that the field of honour should be exchanged for the valley of Sorek. Hence an abundant crop of evil. It was not the Philistines, it was impure passion that extinguished the discernment of Samson. He never saw any object clearly after he went to Gaza and saw an harlot. It is true he saw Delilah, but probably through the obscurity of nocturnal hours. Of her arts, of her perils, he surely had but imperfect vision. Hoodwinked by pleasure, he could not see the seven locks of his head scattered on the toilet of a wanton. The scissors of a gipsey proved sharper than the sword of enemies; and the flowing hair of the hero, once covered with laurel, is now tortured into meretricious ringlets, or periwigs some pimp in Delilah's antechamber.

Genius, said the amiable clergyman with whom I studied divinity, is invariably connected with strong passions. When men, exquisitely organized, indulge pleasure, it is with that species of fervour noted in the oriental page; it is with all their hearts, and with all their soul, and with all their strength, and with all their mind. The insensible lounger, the self-engrossed coxcomb may sleep upon the knees of Delilah and wake again to puny life. But of that opiate of joy, of that golden cup of abomination which the harlot presents, if *you* sip, man of feeling, you will "drain the chalice to the lowest and foulest dregs." Keep the high and safe ground; beware of sliding down the slope of pleasure. It conducts you to some vale of Sorek beneath whose roses are the serpent and the dagger. Go up to Parnassus and see the Muse; an excursion to Gaza to see a mortal beauty is not half so exhilarating.

XII

On Hospitality

"And the old man said, peace be with thee; howsoever let all thy wants lie upon me; only lodge not in the street."—*Judges* xix. 20.

IN an early epoch in the Jewish history, in those good natured days when there was no king in Israel, an enamoured Levite undertook a journey to reclaim a wandering concubine. He had better success than lovers in general when in pursuit of a false fair. For though she proved wanton and had forsaken her keeper, yet he found her at length, not in a bagnio, but in her father's house and, more wonderful still, willing to return to her first love. This ardent youth, who appears to be a genuine son of Adam, remains five days in high spirits at Bethlehem-Judah, drinking with the courteous father and courting an agreeable girl, without once reflecting upon her infidelity or her capricious retreat. He found her once more kind and as charming as ever, and therefore resolves, in the spirit of a most rational philosophy, not to mar the joy of the hour by repiningly adverting to the past.

Still, however, he is not unmindful of his rural tenement on the side of Mount Ephraim. Man is never more happy than when at home, with all his little comforts about him; and home never appears more eligible than when we have found some companion to whom we can point out the prospect of our own acres.

This was precisely the case with our Levite. On the commencement of his journey we may, without violence, imagine that he thought it would probbaly prove inauspicious. Whether the female who had fled would ever return, was a matter of the utmost incertitude. But when, from this painful state of suspense he is relieved by the smiles of the fair fugitive, the exclamation of propitiated love must be: "What rapture to have you restored to Mount Ephraim and to me."

No one appears to rejoice more in this reconciliation than the father of the fickle damsel. At the first interview, we read, he rejoiced to meet the Levite. The whole scene is a pretty picture of the simple but sincere hospitality of primeval times. Every morning the son prepares to depart, and the father urges to stay; and with such persuasive importunity doth he invite to tarry all night and let the heart be merry, that he must have been a sulky Israelite who would not talk, and cheerfully too, for five nights with such a benevolent old gentleman.

Now I hear thee, thou uncharitable sceptic, assert that this was selfish hospitality; that the man of Bethlehem-Judah, anxious to be free from the freaks of a gadding girl, was willing to conciliate the son-in-law; that she herself was an artful coquette, and prompted her sire to treat her lover well for mercenary purposes. I hear from thee many such cold hypotheses. Luckily for the Levite, none of his entertainers in his romantic journey were unbelievers. They viewed him sincere and affectionate, as he appeared. He found from them kindness, soft words, and plenteous fare. That this was true may be seen, even by the disciple of Pyrrho, if he will journey on a little farther with the sojourner of Mount Ephraim.

On the return of the reconciled lovers, evening approaching, their servant, timid from impending night and obscurity, advises to halt and lodge in Jebus, a city of the vicinage. The Levite, with the sentiment of nationality, prefers accommodation in Gibeah, a city of Benjamin, one of the tribes. The benighted travellers find themselves there unknowing and unknown. Without shelter, weary and desolate, they find no seat except in the street, "for there was no man that took them into his house to lodging."

And behold, there came an old man from his work. He is described as returning from his fields at even, like any other tired mortal; some of the eastern writers would have sublimed his beneficence and called him the Genius of Hospitality.

But his actions gave him the best title. When he saw forlorn strangers wandering without a home, he proposes the quick and impatient question, "Whither goest, and whence comest thou!" When told the little story of a Levite's adventures, that he was wayfaring home, and that though he was provided with all necessaries, no one of the citizens would receive him into his house, or suffer him to toast his bread, or warm his wine at the fire—what

is the reply?—Was it that of a morose old man willing to escape from the suspicious or wearisome narrative of a stranger? No; the first accents were peace, and friendship, and invitation:
"Let all thy wants lie upon me, only lodge not in the street."

All the compliments that a voluble Frenchman repeats are as "sounding brass" to the pure gold of genuine Hospitality. She stands, kind power, like the wisdom of Solomon, at the gates, and at the coming in at the doors, and courteously invites us to come in. Her language is kind, not formal; her gestures are few but expressive. In the bad days of this stormy world, it is she who cherishes with the warm garment and warmer welcome.

Be careless, ye pilgrims of the day, where ye wander, or on what coast ye are thrown; if ye can discern hospitality in the street of a strange city, or on the strand where ye have been wrecked, I will promise a short oblivion to your woes. Like the tender host of the Levite, she will make your hearts merry with her cordial wine; she will feed even the dog that follows ye. She will speak peace to the houseless wayfarer; she will say, in the beauty of scriptural language, "Behold the day groweth to an end; lodge not in the street; lodge here, that thine heart may be merry, and to-morrow get you early on your way that thou mayest go home."

XIII

On the Story of Nature

"And he spake of trees, from the cedar tree that is in
Lebanon, even unto the hyssop that springeth out of the
wall: he spake also of beasts, and of fowls, and of
creeping things, and of fishes."—*I Kings* iv. 33.

THE historian of the Jewish kings, in his life of Solomon, after describing him potent abroad, peaceful at home, and magnificent in the palace, concludes with an eulogium upon his wisdom,
adding, as proof, his skill in the various topics of natural history.
The ambitious tree, the grovelling shrub, the lion, the mole, the
volant, the creeping, and the swimming tribes had all been subject
to his researches. The Buffon and the St. Pierre of Israel, he
could narrate the striking beauties of organized matter with the
eloquence of the one, and feel with the sentiment of the other.
Though the cares of state administration were many, yet he would
find or create opportunities to exchange the council board for the
country, and prefer to the study of politics, the study of plants. In
the wood and in the field, the picturesque of nature would charm
more than the tapestry of his palace; and as he roamed with the
fair Egyptian of Pharaoh's race, he might note, both as a philosopher and lover, the coo of the dove, the buds of the pomegranate,
the frolicsome kids, and the ruby rose.

In several parts of these fugitive papers, I have already and
warmly insisted on the advantages of a taste for natural beauty.
This is a Venus de Medicis universally to be found. Italian con-
noisseurs may saunter through the galleries of Florence, admiring
animated canvas or symmetrical marble. I do not wish to vilify
their pursuit. If it be lounging, it is of a liberal sort. I would
not only love the poet and the painter, but the candid critic of
their works. But landscape, described in a poem or mimicked on
the walls, cannot compare with the real glories of nature. Her
trees, her animals, her wood and water, her broken and cultivated
ground, her fish that swiftly glide or her insects which tardily
creep, were the objects that once interested a great prince, and

[141]

ought now to interest those who, like him, would be observing, moral, and wise.

Get up early, then, to the vineyard, and see if the vine flourish and the tender grape appear. Mark the progress of vegetation; observe the characters and habitudes of animals; trace the forest. It has more curious scenery than a theatre. Let the eye of admiration be now raised to the top of the cedar, and now depressed to the hillock of the ant. The nest of the bird and the haunt of the trout, trifling as to the inconsiderate they may appear, will reward a philosophic scrutinizer of nature's operations with abundant and perennial pleasure. Swammerdam, a patient naturalist, has been derided by the levity of sciolists for speculating long and intently upon the lowest subjects of the animal kingdom. The censure was sudden and weak. He was always innocently, often usefully and honorably employed.

The love of nature is a sweet and exhilarating passion. He who botanizes on the mountain or explores the latent root in the forest is a healthy and happy man. To the fiercer gales of life the soldier, the mariner, and the cit are exposed. But if the secure quiet of Virgil be the lot of mortals, it certainly is his whose ambition soars not above the cedar, and whose avarice digs not below the hyssop.

XIV

On Fretfulness

"Doest thou well to be angry for the gourd?"—*Jonah* iv. 9.

OR to fret at any of the petty accidents of life? Thou discontented mortal, undoubted descendant from Jonah and his peevish tribe, why doest thou suffer a cloud to gather on thy brow, because there is a little one, no bigger than a man's hand, rising in the sky? Be serene thyself, and it will import little whether it rains or blows.

Of all vile habits, that of fretfulness is the least tolerable. Many offensive things which vulgar people do are sometimes laid aside, and their neighbours are occasionally freed from annoy. But fretfulness is a kind of perpetual motion, excited no less by a creaking door than a fit of the gout. It is a voracious monster and feeds upon minute as well as vast vexation. Let us strive, therefore, to pluck off this blister from the heart, and even in the hottest and most oppressive days of life, care not whether the shelter of a "gourd" be extended over us or taken away. I have always grieved, ever since the schoolmistress bid me read with a loud voice Jonah's journey to Nineveh, that the prophet should chafe like a roused brute of the forest because a gourd, a short-lived plant of the night, had wilted. It appears to me, even if the sun beat fiercely upon his head and the east wind blew sharply upon his breast, that the prophet might have found so much alleviation of his misfortunes in beholding sixteen thousand people, and "also much cattle," spared from destruction, that a dead gourd would not have given him the spleen. I cannot help feeling a degree of indifference, and perhaps aversion, towards this fretting messenger to the Ninevites. I have a profound respect for all, and a warm affection for most of the other prophets. Many were courtly as well as ingenious writers. I admire the sublimity of Isaiah, the sensibility of Jeremiah, and the generous zeal of Ezekiel. Even the lowly Amos, the herdman of Tekoah, though the narrowness of his education has induced a degree of rudeness in his writings, still I be-

[143]

lieve to be as honest a prophet as ever uttered a prediction. But as for Jonah, setting aside his disobedience, selfishness, and vanity, he was so sulky and so morose a mortal that I never could like his character or his principles. I am not so uncharitable as to wish that he had actually been digested by the whale which swallowed him, but he ought to have kept no better company, for not the "great Leviathan of the deep" ever floundered more impatiently in his element than discontented Jonah in the voyage of life.

On a review of what I have thus far written, I believe that there is no occasion to look so far back as the history of an ancient prophet for an instance of anger employed upon trifles. If I should lift the window-sash of my study, I should discern whole companies fretting and fuming for the "gourd."

Walking in a studious mood by the side of a neighbour's garden fence, I observed him stamping upon the ground with such disorder that I concluded he was in convulsions, or practicing a dance of St. Vitus. Humanity urged me towards him, and I meditated medical rather than moral aid. But to my eager question of "What aileth thee?" he replied, to my astonishment, that the bugs had blighted all his cucumbers, and was not that enough to make a wise man mad? I endeavoured to compose his perturbated spirits, and quoted to him Seneca upon tranquility of mind, and part of one of Basil's homilies, but all in vain. He appeared to be possessed, and it required an abler exorcist than myself to drive his devil away. I retired, and thinking of Jonah and his "gourd," could not help allegorizing a little in Bunyan's manner. My neighbour Irritable's forefathers quoth I, probably cultivated cucumbers without the wall of Nineveh; they fretted when the fruit was cut off, and my worthy friend here, I find, has not yet been cured of the family taint!

XV

On Disappointment

"Wherefore, when I looked that it should bring forth grapes,
brought it forth wild grapes?"—*Isa.* v. 4.

THUS fares it with most of the vineyards in the world. Dressed by the vintager, they promise plausibly as a courtier. In the season of maturity, what is the fruit? When we looked for perfection, we found our hopes mocked with wildness, crudity, bitterness, with fruit austere as sloes, or sour, like the berries of the gadding barberry.

The poet Isaiah, for the prophet, no less than Homer, merits the title of bard, has beautifully allegorized the common disappointments of man. He describes his beloved as the proprietor of a vineyard in a champaign country. Well fenced, well planted, freed from stones, protected by a tower, and crowned by a wine press, such a vineyard might inspire the owner with the fondest expectations of pressing sweet fruit and of drinking the purest nectar. Mortified Hebrew, I see thee walk away with anguish. At autumnal noon thou hast met the vine-dresser, and he has told thee of blight, and mildew, and caterpillar; that the grapes are wild, acid, their juice vinegar; that the vineyard is no better than a thistle field, and thy time and money wasted without recompense. I hear thee, in the bitterness of thy heart, exclaim, "What could have been done more to my vineyard, that I have not done in it?" It is natural. Many a parent has spoken in the same language when hearing of the sorry adventures of a prodigal son. Where men have lavished wealth, hours, affection, whether in rearing grapes or offspring, if either prove wild, it is like a dart through the liver.

Wild grapes, in the sense which the prophet intends, are "as plenty as blackberries." Hoyden girls, forward boys, and dissipated men are all wild grapes. Parents may dress, and schoolmasters prune as much as they please; all culture is in vain where there is rottenness at root and heart.

[145]

The banks of many a western lake, and the savannahs of Georgia and Tennessee have been converted by land-jobbers into vineyards more productive than those of Bourdeaux or Burgundy. Emigrant and eager vintagers have looked for the fruit of their labours and expected to behold high-piled baskets and flasks by the dozen. Such vineyards have yielded prodigiously; barren sand and bankruptcy have been the wild grapes which set the speculator's teeth on edge. Very sour, unpalatable fruits, too hard of digestion even for an ostrich.

The French, for a succession of ages blest with fertile vineyards and crowned with chaplets, were a merry people. In an evil hour, the rage of improvement urged them to grub up that mantling vine which had so long proved

"From storms a shelter, and from heat a shade,"

and to plant certain bastard slips, called trees of liberty. Over the whole kingdom they threw a shade more mournful than yew or cypress. Great expectations have been entertained of the fruit of these trees; but, it is said, noblemen and gentlemen of taste declare nothing can be more "wild," and even the poor peasant shakes his head at the forced production and mawkish flavour of the fruits of liberty, and sighs for a grape or filbert from the gardens of St. Cloud or the Tuilleries.

XVI

Ingratitude of Republics

"For the workman is worthy of his meat."—*Matt.* x. 10.

IF there be such a personage as Truth, this assertion certainly belongs to her family, for what can be more just than that a vintager should eat some, at least, of those grapes which he had planted and watered.

But judging from the practice of the world at the present time, one would think my text was grown obsolete and that its principle was not recognized. In the shambles there is always meat enough, but how little is bestowed upon workmen. Parasites, buffoons, fiddlers, equestrians, French philosophers, and speculators gormandize; but I see Merit, that excellent workman that needeth not to be ashamed, as lank and as lean as my old tabby cat, who has had nothing to eat but church-mice for a year.

Though I am not saluted a brother by any legitimate parson, and belong to no ministerial association on earth, yet I cherish great respect and feel a cordial regard for the established clergy. I consider them, with few exceptions, as faithful workmen; they make us moral, they instruct our youth, they lead sober and peaceable lives.

"Along the cool, sequestered vale of life,
They keep the noiseless tenor of their way."

They are wise, they are amiable men, though they are ignorant of foolish questions and "strivings about the law;" they understand perfectly the great rules of life. Such men, therefore, are worthy of their meat, and should be liberally provided. They labour much: few men labour more; they are compelled to exercise not only the head but the hands. The private estate, as well as the gospel vineyard, claims their care. When the drudgery of the year is done, when numerous sermons have been composed and numersick-chambers visited, when they have been in watchings and weariness often, what meat will the benevolence of a parish bestow? Verily, a morsel. A beggarly pittance, called a salary, and that pittance scantily and grudgingly paid. When I visit a village covered with stores and shops and cultivated by opulent farmers; when I hear the inhabitants boast of their flourishing circumstances and recount how many bushels of wheat they threshed last year, and how well it sold; if I should be informed that their parson's annual stipend is but sixty pounds, in despite of all their boasted riches and ostentation, I should think them unworthy to enter a church.

If I should repair to any place where men congregate and describe to them one who, in an hour of jeopardy, had quitted his hearth, travelled many wearisome miles, been exposed to sickly air, been shot at for hours, and frequently without a crust or a draught to supply the waste of nature; if I should add that all this peril was sustained that we, at home, might live in security, not one of my audience, provided speculators and bloodsuckers were not of the number, would deny, that the old soldier was a worthy workman. But where is his meat? Oh, my good sir, do not propose that question in a republic; you know that a republic is never bounteous. Belisariuses ask for their obolus here, as well as at Rome. But here the business ends. They *receive*, in Great Britain and elsewhere. You might as soon expect moderation in a Frenchman, or knowledge of the belles lettres in a country attorney, as that a *commonwealth* should be grateful.

XVII

On Cleanliness

"Let thy garments be always white; and let thy head
lack no ointment."—*Eccl.* ix. 8.

THOUGH much occupied in preaching and noted, as some of
my friends say, for a certain poetical heedlessness of character, yet
if not oftener, at least every Sunday, I copy the common custom
and invest my little person in clean array. As from a variety of
motives, and none of them, I hope, bad ones, I go with some degree of constancy to church, I choose to appear there decently and
in order. However inattentive through the week, on the solemn
day I brush with more than ordinary pains my best coat, am
watchful of the purity of my linen, and adjust my cravat with an
old bachelor's nicety. While I was lately busied at my toilet, in
the work of personal decoration, it popped into my head that a
sermon in praise of neatness would do good service, if not to the
world at large, at least to many of my reading, writing, and
thinking brethren, who make their assiduous homage to mind a
pretext for negligence of person.

Among the minor virtues, cleanliness ought to be conspicuously
ranked; and in the common topics of praise we generally arrange
some commendation of neatness. It involves much. It supposes a
love of order, an attention to the laws of custom, and a decent
pride. My Lord Bacon says that a good person is a perpetual letter of recommendation. This idea may be extended. Of a well-
dressed man it may be affirmed that he has a sure passport
through the realms of civility. In first interviews we can judge
of no one, except from appearances. He, therefore, whose exter-
ior is agreeable begins well in any society. Men and women are
disposed to augur favourably, rather than otherwise, of him who
manifests by the purity and propriety of his garb a disposition to
comply and to please. As in rhetoric a judicious exordium is of
admirable use to render an audience docile, attentive, and benevolent, so at your introduction into good company, clean and modish

[149]

apparel is, though an humble, at least a serviceable herald of our exertions.

As these are very obvious truths, and as literary men are generally vain and sometimes proud, it is singular that one of the easiest modes of gratifying self-complacency should, by them, be for the most part neglected; and that this sort of carelessness is so adhesive to one tribe of writers that the words poet and sloven are regarded as synonymous in the world's vocabulary.

This negligence in men of letters sometimes arises from their inordinate application to books and papers, and may be palliated by a good-natured man as the natural product of a mind too intensely engaged in sublime speculations to attend to the blackness of a shoe, or the whiteness of a ruffle. Mr. Locke and Sir Isaac Newton might be forgiven by their candid contemporaries, though the first had composed his essay with "unwashen hands," and the second had investigated the laws of nature when he was clad in a soiled night-gown. But slovenliness is often affected by authors, or rather pretenders to authorship, and must then be considered as highly culpable, as an outrage of decorum, as a defiance to the world, and as a pitiful scheme to attract notice by means which are equally in the power of the drayman and the chimney sweeper. I know a poet of this description, who anticipates renown no less from a dirty shirt than from an elegant couplet, and imagines that when his appearance is the most sordid, the world must conclude, of course, that his mind is splendid and fair. In his opinion, "marvellous foul linen" is a token of wit, and inky fingers indicate humour; he avers that a slouched hat is demonstrative of a well-stored brain and that genius always trudges about in unbuckled shoes. He looks for invention in rumpled ruffles and finds high-sounding poetry among the folds of a loose stocking. But this smirched son of Apollo may be assured there is no necessary connexion between dirt and ability. It is not necessary to consummate such a marriage to produce the fairest offspring of the mind. One may write brilliantly and, strange as it may seem, be dressed well. If negligence be the criterion of genius, a critic will, in future, inspect a poet's wardrobe rather than his works. Slovenliness, so far from being commendable in an author, is more inexcusable in men of letters than in many others, the nature of whose employment compels them to be conversant with objects sordid and impure. A smith from his forge, or a husbandman from his field, is obliged sometimes to appear stained with the smut of the one, or the dust of the other. A writer, on the contrary, sitting in an easy chair at a polished desk and leaning on white paper or examining the pages of a book, is by no means obliged to be sordid by his labours. I see no reason why an author should not be a gentleman, or at least as clean and neat as a Quaker. Far from thinking that filthy dress marks a liberal mind, I should suspect the good sense and talents of him who affected to wear a tattered coat as the badge of his profession. Should I see a reputed genius totally regardless of his person, I should immediately doubt the delicacy of his taste and the accuracy of his judgment. I should conclude there was some obliquity in his mind, a dull sense of decorum, and a disregard of order. I should fancy that he consorted with low society; and instead of claiming the privilege of genius to knock and be admitted at palaces, that he chose to sneak in at the back door of hovels, and wallow brutishly in the sty of the vulgar.

It is recorded of Somerville and Shenstone that they were negligent, and of Smith that he was a sloven. But disregard of dress is by no means a constant trait in the literary character. Edmund Waller, Prior, Swift, and Bolingbroke were remarkably neat in their persons and curious in the choice of apparel; and of David Mallet, Dr. Johnson observes "that his appearance was agreeable, and he suffered it to want no recommendation that dress could give."

The orientals are careful of their persons, with much care. Their frequent ablutions and change of garments are noticed in every page of their history. My next text is not the only precept of neatness that can be quoted from the Bible. The wise men of the East supposed there was some analogy between the purity of the body and the mind, nor is this a vain imagination.

I cannot conclude this sermon better than by an extract from the works of Count Rumford, who, in few and strong words, has fortified my doctrine:

"With what care and attention do the feathered race wash themselves and put their plumage in order; and how perfectly neat, clean, and elegant do they ever appear. Among the beasts of the field, we find that those which are the most cleanly are generally the most gay and cheerful, or are distinguished by a certain air of tranquility and contentment; and singing birds are always remarkable for the neatness of their plumage." So great is the effect of cleanliness upon man that it extends even to his moral character. Virtue never dwelt long with filth; nor do I believe there ever was a person scrupulously attentive to cleanliness who was a consummate villain.

XVIII

Story of Jacob

"In the morning behold it was Leah."—*Gen.* xxix. 25.

THIS, as Macbeth says, inspecting his crimsoned hand in the play, was a "sorry sight" to the luckless Jacob. From the "blear eyes" of an unexpected bride, the gazing patriarch could discern reflected no very charming prospect of matrimonial felicity.

Without anticipating too soon the reflections, or fancying the chagrin, of the injured Jacob, it is better to narrate certain of his youthful bargains, describe his apprenticeship or rather vassalage to Love, and sketch a picture of the sanguine hopes and abused credulity of a young man.

Jacob, the favourite son of a fond mother, is advised by Rebekah, terrified at the hatred and menaces of Esau, to flee from the effects of fraternal resentment and to lurk for a time in the obscurity of Haran, a remote village in the East, where he would not only find the safe shelter of solitude but the still more friendly cover of a relation's love. Haran was a sweet and pastoral country, amidst whose delicious landscapes he could lose, or at least suspend, the recollection of domestic misfortunes. Haran was the abode of Laban, an uncle and a friend. If the terrors of a brother's vengeance were not lost amid the glories of nature and the charms of sylvan life, they would be mitigated by the kindness, they might be braved by the strength, of a relative and a pastoral chieftain. Jacob, who had most unjustifiably defrauded Esau of his father's benediction, was sufficiently alarmed for his own safety to discern the correctness of this reasoning. He immediately commences his tour, arrives at his asylum, "the land of the people of the east," and suddenly finds himself among a company of shepherds busied in watering their flocks. This was the very scene for a love adventure, and it immediately occurs. Inquiring of this simple company with the friendly zeal, or perhaps the rude curiosity, of a New England man, where they belonged, &c. he is answered that they are inhabitants of Haran, that they know Laban, that he is in health, and that "behold Rachel, his daughter, cometh with the sheep." This fair girl next appears; and after certain civilities and gallantries of Jacob, which mark the honesty, simplicity, and tenderness of undebauched manners and pastoral times, he informs the damsel, with whom he is suddenly enamoured, of their affinity; and the youthful admirer of Rachel is announced to the son of Nahor. Laban hastens to meet his fugitive nephew, and with apparent frankness and cordiality brings him to his house. In a month Jacob becomes wholly domesticated in this family. At length, this avaricious Jew, in a spirit of speculation not unworthy of the present age, begins to drive an artful bargain with his unsuspecting inmate. After insidiously hinting that the ties of consanguinity ought not induce him to a gratuitous service, Laban demands his price, and the generous and lovesick swain replies, "Your daughter." It must here be noted that Laban had two daughters, and that there was no small difference in their personal attractions, for "Leah was tender eyed, but Rachel was beautiful and well favoured." Now I will not torment myself and puzzle my readers with the different and jarring explanation of grave commentators, defining the epithet applied to Leah. From the opposition of the clauses, it is extremely clear that one of the damsels was homely, the other exquisitely beautiful. Jacob chose like a lover, and conducted like a very fond one. He prefers Rachel, and stipulates for a septennial servitude as the price of her father's consent and her affection. Laban replies, in a blunt and Squire Western style, that it was better that Jacob should have her than anybody else; and the contract is made. Notwithstanding the extreme length of this period of amorous probation, to the captivated youth it seemed, in the charming language of the original, but a few days, for the love he had to her. A modern lover would have been tired in seven days, but every vicissitude of seven years found Jacob's heart the same. Of this prolix courtship, the last day, a day of jubilee to love, at length is numbered. Jacob claims his wife. Laban ostentatiously invites his neighbours, and the wedding banquet and bridal couch are spread. The knavery of Jacob's unworthy uncle now appears. During the gaiety of nuptial carousals, when the head of an ardent bridegroom would, in some degree, dance to the bounding of his heart, and in the obscurity of nocturnal hours, a surreptitious consort is treacherously conveyed to his apartment. The dawn reveals the cheat to insulted fondness, for in the morning—behold it was Leah.

"Ye who listen with credulity to the whispers of Fancy, and pursue with eagerness the phantoms of hope," learn to be on your guard against the cheating Labans of life and rely not too implicitly on the expectation of clasping the Rachel of your joys. Ye know not what a night and the cunning craftiness of man may bring forth. Some unlucky accident may rush between you and expected bliss. Think not, good easy men, when ye sleep and dream of delight, that the powers of deception are nodding too. No, they are broad awake, and perhaps maliciously active. See, they are already busy, detaining your Rachel, and in the morning ye must be doomed to disappointment and perceive nothing but a Leah for your consolation.

Thwarted passion is always like a dart through the liver. But disappointments in love are like a whole quiver. They terribly lacerate the feeling heart. Of all the sufferers in this way, the hapless Jacob, I think, was the greatest. Violently enamored with a lovely shepherdess, he has not only to obtain the "slow leave" of a timid virgin, but must toil for the tardy and remote consent of a miserly sire. To this irksome and ignominious exaction Jacob submits. He "fed the sheep, and penned the fold," and bartered severe labour for the smiles of love. He at length rests from the toil of years, and is defrauded of the beauteous premium.

We all know from the context how well Jacob behaved under the stinging disappointment. After a concise but pointed remonstrance to his uncle, he calms the tulmult of desire and for the love of his betrothed, promises Laban to set out, like the shepherd swain of *Lycidas*,

"To-morrow to fresh fields and pastures new."

There is an excellent moral to be drawn from the story; and if among my readers any of the more ardent and unsuspicious suffer from a Laban, and love like Jacob, let them copy the resignation of a patient man, and wait seven years longer for gratification rather than be enraged or dejected for a month, or even a day.

[155]

XIX

Story of Ruth

"And it came to pass, when they were come to Bethlehem, that all the city was moved about them, and they said, Is this Naomi?"—*Ruth* i. 19.

NOW what was there peculiar in the character, or eventful in the fortunes of this woman, to excite such a general commotion in one of the most populous cities of Judah? Probably she was a lady of exalted rank, perhaps a king's daughter or some unfortunate empress whose woes, like those of injured Antoinette, claimed the pity not only of a city but of the world. Thus, impatient Curiosity, art thou wont to hurry to erroneous conclusions. I am weary of thy conjectures. The book of Ruth shall end them.

Ah, the book of Ruth. But what can be learned from a tale so simple, which Thomas Paine has called an idle, bundling story? Believe me, ye among my readers who have heads of fancy and hearts of feeling, that notwithstanding the deistical effrontery and impious vulgarism of that renegado, the book of Ruth is a specimen of fine writing and of amiable morality, not often to be found. It is a drama, too; and trust me that neither Euripides, nor Sophocles, nor even the magical Shakspeare ever conceived or expressed scenes more tender than the wife and daughter of Elimelech personated in the highway of Moab and among the reapers of Boaz.

During the judicial administration of Judah, a famine compelled a man of Bethlehem, his wife and sons to migrate to Moab. The wife soon became a widow. This forlorn female, alone in the land of strangers, her little estate impoverished, seeing the partner of her cares and the hope of her age extinct, and hearing that the fields of Bethlehem were once more fertile, prepared to return, in a state of mournful expectation, to her native land. And was there no kind-hearted and sociable spirit to attend thee, O Naomi, in this thy pensive pilgrimage, to lend thee a supporting arm and to wipe the tears of a poor widow? Was every Moabite so inhumane as to be unmindful of an unfortunate stranger? Could not thy drooping age find at least one staff from the remnants of the broken house of Elimelech? Yes, there was an Orpah to kiss away the tears of dejection—there was a Ruth to follow wherever a mourning mother should lead.

Now, although in the days of my youth and fantasy I have wandered whole nights, delighted, among the fairy fictions of the Arabian tales; although I read ten times the adventures of Don Quixote, lunatic Knight, and of Gulliver, sober-faced seaman; although I have followed with anxious eyes John Bunyan's Christian, whether rising the hill Difficult, or wading the slough Despond, yet never have I read a novel of more interest or purer simplicity than this oriental historiette.

The affectionate maiden whose name is the title of the story "clave" to Naomi, and insisted to be her fellow traveller, notwithstanding her most eager and earnest remonstrances. Their contests were friendly, and pleasant will it be to narrate them. To dissuade Ruth from this journey, Naomi employed forcible arguments addressed to the passions of a young woman, addressed to vanity and to love. She told her that, as her sister Orpah chose to remain in Moab, it would be better to abide there as her companion. In her own country Ruth could meet many lovers and friends; in another, every face would be a strange one, and probably every heart would be cold. But neither the expostulation of an experienced matron, nor the dread of poverty, nor of beauty neglected, could frustrate the benevolent purpose of this amiable young woman. For she said, "Entreat me not to leave thee, or to return from following after thee; for whither thou goest, I will go; and where thou lodgest, I will lodge."

Such a determination must be approved by a fond parent; that it was so, appears from the expressive silence of Naomi and from the context, for "they two went until they came to Bethlehem." This was verily *a sentimental journey;* it might be entitled "The Travels of the Charities," and be likened unto the kissing of Righteousness and Peace.

But in such a journey there could be but few incidents. The hearts of Naomi and of her daughter were too full for utterance; if I were disposed to record the language of their looks I might protract a prolix sermon. It is needless. Every son of sensibility knows what kind of dialogue would pass between maternal affection and filial gratitude.

[157]

However silent these pilgrims might be themselves, it seems that others talked, and loudly too, at the sight of virtue and beauty in distress. For we read that it came to pass, when they were come to Bethlehem, that all the city was moved about them, and they said, "Is this Naomi?"

This brings me to a main design of this discourse. My impatient readers, fretting at the desultory Lay Preacher, think, doubtless, that I have wandered from my way. Perhaps this is a correct opinion, but all except Dutch divines will leave the narrow and strait path of method for the sake of a ramble with such agreeable personages as I have been describing.

"All the city was moved about them, and they said, 'Is this Naomi?' " What, a whole metropolis commiserating the distresses of two obscure females! Then it seems that men can flock together in the market place for other purposes than those of gain. A city was in commotion, but not from eagerness to resort to the tables of the money changer or the seats of those who sold doves. A city was in commotion, not because the enemy was without the gates or the police disturbed within. A city was in commotion, and thousands were anxious, because two fellow mortals were unhappy.

An English philosopher, an English physician, and a French duke have strongly asserted, in their respective works, that the natural state of man was warfare, and that he is invariably a selfish animal. Away with such philosophy. If this be truth let me always grope in error. As the philanthropic Sterne declares, we are not stocks and stones; and though I detest dreary metaphysics, I can believe with Dr. Hartley in the doctrine of vibrations. It is a doctrine of humanity, and every man of Bethlehem-Judah understood it well when he surveyed with trickling tears the return of Naomi. Though the "bold bad men" of this world insist that pity is synonymous with contempt, I pray you, my benevolent readers, never to consult their dictionary. When an afflicted sister or brother knocks, let the gates of charity be thrown wide open. Like the sympathizing city of old, be "moved" at a picture of misfortune. To the Naomis of this world, give "beauty for ashes," and provide a benevolent Boaz for every virtuous Ruth.

XX

On the Sabbath

"When will the new moon be gone that we may sell corn? and the sabbath, that we may set forth wheat?"—*Amos* viii. 5.

IN the dissipated cities of London and Edinburgh, the abuse of Sunday has been a common theme of reproach among those weekly guardians of the public virtue, the perodical essayists. Johnson and Hawksworth heard the turbulence of a riot and the roar of intoxication from the saloons and taverns of the capital, but their confidence in the innocence or the piety of the villagers precluded even the faint inquiry whether holy days were profaned by rustics. Moralists might repair to the hamlet on week-days and remark vice and folly; but on the sabbath, the young and the old, the careless and the regular, would be found nowhere but in a church.

Though the catholic spirit of the age of reason indulge the latitudinarian with an immunity from Sabbath formalities, still it might be imagined there could be found, both in town and country, men who, if they did not kneel at the altar, would sit decently and seriously at the fireside. Libertines might be averse to hear a sermon or make a response, yet not wish a Sunday away, that they might set forth wheat, the bottle, or card table.

This, however, experience proves a vain imagination. The seventh day is observed by multitudes, neither as a season of worship nor rest. The country and the city are alike neglectful. On Sunday the husbandman often examines his crops, the merchant computes interest, the rake urges his steed, and the attorney draws his declaration.

This impatience of a day sacred to quiet and piety is an odd trait in the character of those who are saluted with the title of rational. Man is such an indolent being, we are not surprised that he declines the exercises of Sunday but that he loathes its rest. Of many loungers whom I know, I have computed, with mathematical precision, the yawns on every Sunday and Monday, through the year. I find that the aggregate lassitude of the former to the latter is as ten to one.

The watch is fretfully consulted and its owner querulously asks why tarry its wheels, why does the dial-point so tardily indicate the twilight hour?

Although the custom of going to church is ancient, honourable, and from social and political, as well as moral and religious reasons, laudable, yet as my liberal scheme never excludes from the pale of charity one who prefers retired to ostentatious devotion, I am desirous of convincing the loiterer at home on the Sabbath that there is no reason for abolishing or abbreviating that tranquil day. It is better to go up with the Israelites to the temple, but still a domestic Sunday may be useful and pious if correctly improved, and if we do not absurdly wish it away. The apostle prescribes "milk for babes." The moralist good-naturedly allows some squeamish ones the indulgence of a vitiated devotional taste and suggests a pleasant and practicable regimen.

It must, however, be peremptorily required that no immoral querist ask when the Sabbath will be gone that he may sell corn, set forth wheat, or attend to any low and secular cares. If he stay from church, let him not grieve the Sunday. If he will not sing with the organ, let him not play on the violin.

That Sunday may delectably pass, it is not necessary that cocks should fight, bowls be quaffed, or bargains be made. The seventh day is like a hermit who not only utters the orison and numbers beads but loves the "studious nook" and the lonely scene. Nothing militating, therefore, with order and peace should be tolerated. The jovial cry may be raised, and "quips and cranks" uttered at "the time to laugh;" but the grave and the composed style suits the sobriety of the Sabbath.

Lest the gayer department of my readers should think I envelope the Christian day in funeral weeds and tragic pall, I will strive to convince by my conclusion that pleasure and piety, like the Hermia and Helena of the poet, may "sing one song, both in one key."

The man who has toiled or idled six days may, on the morning of the seventh, choose a retired walk, avoiding the highway and offence to the weaker brother. I will not be so puritanical or unfashionable as to hint that the vista of this walk should be a fane or a chapel. The contemplation of the sublime and beautiful of nature, vivified "by the regent of the world," will naturally excite, in a good mind, the proper emotion. Of ecstacy or of rant there is no need. The homage of the heart is better than the nasal twang of a whole conventicle.

The forenoon may be devoted to popular theology and to sermons. My airy pupils need not start nor pale. I do not place them in the tutelage of the dozing Gill or the mystical Behmen. I do not place them among Westminster divines or on the Saybrook platform. Privileged with the company of Atterbury, bishop Watson, and Laurence Sterne, they may consider themselves not only in a learned and ingenious, but a polite circle. I shall not be called a sour presbyter by those whom I advise, if I select for their Sunday acquaintance gentlemen as well as Christians.

A dinner with some liberal clergyman, though "a dinner of herbs," will prove a better refection than a corporation feast.

The afternoon will pass without much tedium if employed among a well ordered family and rational friends. At intervals, serious poetry will yield a high delight. The gospel sonnets of Erskine are not recommended, but the moral Young and the enthusiastic Gray.

At the close of such a day, the observer of it will not repine that religion and the laws refuse, once a week, to permit the sowing of wheat or the sale of corn. He will rejoice in this tabernacle of rest, and though delighting, at proper periods, in business and the agitations of life, will not forsake the waters of that Sabbath Siloam which flow softly.

XXI

Interment of Saul

"And when the inhabitants of Jabesh-gilead heard of
that which the Philistines had done to Saul, all the valiant
men arose, and went all night, and took the body of Saul,
and the bodies of his sons, from the wall of Bethshan, and
came to Jabesh, and burnt them there. And they took their
bones, and buried them under a tree at Jabesh, and fasted
seven days."—*I Sam.* xxxi. 11, 12, 15.

DURING my residence at the university, I had the good fortune to attract the notice and enjoy the conversation of a country
clergyman whose brilliant talents neither parochial penuriousness
could choke, nor the shades of rural obscurity conceal. From the
barren uniformity of cloistered life, and the still more arid lessons of solemn pedantry, I used to escape, each vacation, and meet,
at a parsonage, Wit and Learning attired in priestly grey. Here,
after being "long detained, in the obscure sojourn" of a college
cell, I could reascend to the realms of Fancy and "feel the sovereign vital lamp" of Genius. Here I lost my tutors and found a
friend. It was like the exchange of armour between Glaucus and
Diomede; it was brass for gold.

One day, in the study of this liberal Levite, whom I heartily
wish was copied in everything "but his nonconformity," and who
ought to preach in Westminster Abbey rather than in a dissenting
conventicle, I picked up one of his neglected sermons. It was
Shandean, and the eccentric prebendary of York might have bound
it up with his own. As this sermon gave the first hint to that
style of lay preaching which I have for some years employed, as
it was a model of ease and sentiment in alliance, and as its text
was that which I have selected for my present speculation, I could
not deny myself the pleasure of complimenting a curate who deserves to be a bishop; and if there be any merit in the following
thoughts, it is ascribable to him whose elegant homilies "inspired
easy my unpremeditated page." In pursuing this track, I shall be
acquitted of plagiarism when my readers remember my prodigal
use of inverted commas and my care to give credit for borrowed
thought and expression.

But while I am thus wandering, the men of Jabesh-gilead seem to be forgotten. This would be too shameful an act of oblivion. It shall not pass, for they deserve a long and honourable memorial.

The inhabitants of the above oriental village are introduced, with some abruption, to the acquaintance of the student of the book of Samuel. At the very bottom of the first volume of the prophecy, in a kind of postscript to the work, is found the narrative of the funeral rites paid to the family of Saul. Not the smallest reason appears for this posthumous service. On the contrary, it looks not only odd but unmerited, and even impious. For during whole pages immediately preceding this circumstance, we find nothing but a shameful catalogue of Saul's crimes. To bitter envy of the favoured David's talents, he adds a contempt of the ordinances of the Supreme Being and neglect of the mandates of his prophets. In a nocturnal visit to the enchantress of Endor he employs infernal and necromantic arts to disturb the repose of the tomb, and concludes a life of violence, cruelty, and madness by an act of suicide. One would suppose that, in those holy times, the bones of so bad a man would long have been suffered to whiten the mount of Gilboa, and that not even a common sepulture would have been indulged to a body prematurely destroyed by an irreligious prince. Here is a mystery; and on the first view of the inhabitants of Jabesh-gilead, in mourning weeds, under "the wall of Bethshan," we are astonished at their zeal for the interment of this monarch. That all the valiant men of a respectable district should arise and hasten by night to Bethshan, which, it must be observed, was a hostile city in Philistia; that they should take the bones of one whom heaven had abandoned and who had been his own destroyer; that they should expose themselves to the chance of death, or capture, in an enemy's country; that, mocking this terror, and even the still greater one of the vengeance of the skies, they should take the remains of the flagitious Saul and, "with dirges due, and sad array," follow them to the humble *morai* of primaeval burial and deposit them "under a tree" of their own groves; and that the poignancy of their grief should be such as to induce a fast of seven days—all these circumstances are, apparently, the incidents of wild romance or like the adventures of the Venetian Moor. They are "strange, passing strange." But let us develop the occult cause of this conduct and inquire whether these "mourners, going about the streets" of Bethshan, cannot be justified, nay, admired. As they are all valiant men, it is hard to suppose that so shining a virtue as courage should be disgraced by mad and vicious companions. Bravery, like the son of Tobias, is "of a good stock," and when you tell me of a good soldier, I look to see him invested not only with the gorget and sash of military splendour but with the more lustrous ornament of the manly virtues: the mantle of charity and "the breast-plate of righteousness."

Whether this expectation is generally realized or not, it is fully so in the case of the valiant men of the East; and as will immediately appear, their conduct, as simply described by the holy narrator, presents one of the most affecting and honourable instances of political and personal gratitude to be found in the immense tablet of historical composition.

In the eleventh chapter of Samuel we find a clue that guides us, at once, through the labyrinth of the above mystery. At the commencement of Saul's reign, Nahash, a prince of the house of Ammon, whose trade was rapine and blood, waged war with Jabesh-gilead. Its inhabitants propose a treaty of peace, which the haughty invader cruelly proposes to clog with the sanguinary and infamous condition of the extinction of their right eyes. Whether in that early period of their history, the inhabitants were few, defenceless, and incapable of opposing a formidable foe; or their senators, like those which have composed and disgraced more modern councils, were willing to yield to ignominious exaction, is not ascertained. But whether weakness or baseness predominated, it is known that the elders of the country implored the truce of a week; and meanwhile Saul is apprised of their calamitous situation. His subjects wept, and the monarch sympathized. Indignation at the wrongs of his neighbours and pity for their misfortunes dictated a summary and gallant process. He marches against and defeats the Ammonites, and the men of Jabesh retain their freedom.

They were the ancestors of that weeping band whom we have

seen performing a solemn office to the dead. It was during the youth of Saul that he avenged the men of Jabesh upon the Ammonites. Many years had elapsed since this brilliant military exploit, which preserved the eyes and independence of a threatened people. Saul had degenerated from the virtues of his youth, had lost the confidence of an inspired mentor, had forfeited the favour of heaven, had surrendered himself up to vice, had lost an army, and, to add to his disgrace, it was by Philistine soldiers he was conquered, had lost three sons, and finally, losing hope itself, had fallen on his own sword. He is prone on the mountains of Gilboa, without a friend to close his eyes,

"Fallen from his high estate,
And weltering in his blood."

Those whom he had rescued from the Ammonites are all as lifeless as he. Then who is there to mourn for Saul and Jonathan? It was the descendants of those whom Saul had once protected. For when this grateful race heard the melancholy tidings of the defeat and death of the deliverer of their ancestors, what was their arrangement? Was it oblivious of a remote obligation, or did selfishness whisper that an old benefit, like an old hound, was a worthless supernumerary? No; a prompt and noble gratitude appeared, nor did it come alone. It was associated with bravery. "All the valiant men arose." Through the mist of ages I see you, gallant soldiers, your posture erect, but your eyes overflowing. A brave man has, generally, "a tear for pity." You remembered what Saul once was and how he had preserved your progenitors. You forgot nothing but his disgrace and his vices. You had heard that "the battle went sore" against a benefactor, that cruel archers had wounded and the javelin of despair had killed him. You hastened with military and grateful ardour your nocturnal march through a hostile region. You buried the bones of your benefactor, with simple and rustic rites; and the memory of your tears, your respect for the dead, and your fasting, shall never fade away. Sensibility shall erect to your virtue:

"A monument, and plant it round with shade
Of laurel ever green, and branching palm,
With all your trophies hung, and acts inroll'd
In copious legend, or sweet lyric song."

[165]

XXII

Of Precipitation

"And the driving is like the driving of Jehu, the son of
Nimshi; for he driveth furiously."—*2 Kings* ix. 20

NOTHING is to be gained by such excessive speed. It is the
mark of a giddy, hair-brained charioteer. He generally either
breaks his neck, or is distanced in the race by his very eagerness to
reach the goal.

Lord Chesterfield took a distinction between haste and hurry
and, with the precision of a lawyer, marked their dissimilitude.
There is positively as much difference between these pretended
cousin-germans as between my sermons and those of the Archbishop of Canterbury.

Hurry, or as it is called in the text, "driving," is a mischievous
imp, goading us to dash our feet against a stone, to run, with
nightcap on, into the streets; in fine, to be ever slovenly and imperfect. You may dispatch business, but if you hurry it, I will
not ask for the second sight of a Scotchman that I may discover
your approaching bankruptcy.

Young man, I say unto thee, walk gently to riches, to honours,
to pleasure. Do not run. Observe the impatient racer. He is
breathless; he is fallen; bemired and beluted, like Dr. Slop, overthrown by Obadiah; he is distanced; he is hissed. Walk circum-
spectly—it is Paul's advice—not like a fool but like a philosopher.
Compare the man of moderation with the man of impetuosity.
The first becomes honoured in king's courts. The second is either
in jail or in "poverty to the very lips."

In my boyhood, I remember that a parent would sometimes repeat lessons of economy as I sat on his knees, and then lift me in
his arms that I might look at Hogarth's plates of Industry and
Idleness. On youthful fancy the picture was more impressed than
the precept. To relieve that description of my readers who tire
at the didactic and the trite style of morality, I will attempt a
sketch or two, perhaps with a little colouring.

I will imagine the figure of a stripling, educated for business. Seven years he swept and garnished a counting-house; opened it at five, and did not bar it until nine; sold ropes and boxes for himself as well as bales for his master; read "The Sure Guide to Love and Esteem," and worked every rule in Hodder's Arithmetic. This, all must allow, was a gentle pace. No freaks, no starts discompose the placid life of a youth in these habits. Men already look forward and behold him a bank director, or see him in the largest store in the mart.

One ill-omened day, when the moon was full or the dog-star growled, I do not remember which, our sober youth, whose studies were seldom more miscellaneous than an invoice or bill of lading, unluckily had his eye caught by a land advertisement in a newspaper. It will abridge a tedious process of circumstances to imagine him in Georgia. How many acres of sand were then bought and sold, and how he dashed about thy falls, St. Anthony, who art more visited than the shrine of Thomas a Becket! Over these sands he already drives in his chariot, with somebody by his side too:—a lady from Babylon. Although the carriage is encumbered with a speculator, and . . . . . and imaginary bank bills in bales, yet how we glide along, not like the son of Ahimaaz bringing good tidings. The driving is like the charioteership of the son of Nimshi, furious, careless, mad.

But his vehicle, like Count Basset's in the play, rolls on the four aces, or something as unstable. He drives furiously against a post. He is an overthrown Pharaoh, not, as it is vulgarly expressed, in a peck, but in a Red Sea, of troubles. He has driven so furiously that he has snapped his traces, lost the linch-pin and broken the axle of his credit.

A quack is a Jehu; he not only drives furiously himself but he drives his poor patients too. When I see one of these mountebanks I always consider the sick he attends as so many coughing drayhorses, soon to be driven out of breath. Ye simple farmers, why do you grease his wheels? When ye are diseased, cannot a leaf of mugwort be obtained without paying him for the cropping? When you are wounded, your youngest children may bring you a bit of betony, and it will not be charged.

Of the genus of drivers, the negro driver and the impetuous Frenchmen are a noted species. But it does not demand the perspicacity of a watchman to discover their course. They go on at a fearful rate, and it may demand a thunderbolt to arrest either in the impious career.

XXIII

On Scandal

"Study to be quiet, and to do your own business."—*1 Thess.* iv. 11.

THE Thessalonians, to whom this rule was given, were probably an inquisitive race and, like the men of Athens, spent their time in nothing else but either to tell or to hear some new thing. We must frame such a supposition to excuse St. Paul from the charge of impertinence. For nothing can appear more a work of supererogation than to tell man, selfish by nature, to live in peace and to pursue his own advantage. Nature, and the primary laws of being, have told him so already. But this epistle, written at Athens and sent to Thessalonica—that is, from one tattling, idle city to another—was seasonable and proper, notwithstanding all fine reasoning to the contrary. For myself, I can affirm confidently that I need not turn over the archives of the Thessalonians to discover a million of cases where men study to be restless and to pry into other people's business.

Impertinent curiosity is, however, a vice of the village rather than of the city. I am surprised that Paul did not give the direction in the text expressly to the *country* people. For though impertinence is not so local as never to be found except in cottages, still it is a fact that the askers of whys and wherefores are generally villagers, and not cits. In town, strange sights are so common and the tongues of fame so numerous that each inhabitant, distracted with endless variety, thinks it better to mind his own business than to inspect the concerns of a thousand neighbours. In the country, external circumstances being essentially different, the manners of the people assume a different colour; there the incidents are so few on which glutton curiosity can feed that even morsel novelties are seized upon with avidity. A farmer's purchase of a silk gown for his wife, or the irregular pregnancy of his daughter, I have known to engross for weeks the thoughts and chat of those vacant and meddling neighbourhoods which disobey the precept of Paul.

[169]

A certain elegant fabulist among the Latins describes a race of the busy bodies, running wildly about, out of breath with inquiring, prying into every nook, and, by their restless indolence, wearying themselves and tormenting others. This is a strong picture, and some might say, overcharged; a Darly's caricatura of manners rather than the natural strokes of an Italian. But I will engage to find the originals of this portrait in every village I visit. Men in the country, no less than in town, have various schemes to execute and many duties which ought to be discharged. But negligent of these, and with the beam in their own eyes, they go groping about to discover a mote in their neighbour's.—'Tis a *mote*, in general, that they gaze for most earnestly, and it is a mote that they magnify into a mountain.

This weak if not criminal conduct is generally the first begotten of jealousy and rivalship. The malignant inquiries that are then made of a neighbour's fortune or fame are veiled by an affectation of impartiality and candour. But all may discern that such insidious queries are, like arrows discharged from a covert, meant to deeply wound, and yet, by their course, not to betray the archer.

What is it to thee, censorious woman, if thy frail sister have lapsed by the wayside? Doth her fall shake thy foundation, and hast thou to bear the burden of her suckling? Gaze not at her infirmity, nor circulate her reproach. Con over the catalogue of thy own gallantries and, trust me, thou wilt not have a moment left to read or to compile a scandalous chronicle.

What is it to thee, meddling man, if thy neighbour's goods be attached; hast thou to pay the fees of the officer? Keep *thy* ledger accurately, and peep not into his day-book. Ask not of his apprentices how they fare at their master's board, nor how many dollars he takes in a year. Study to be quiet, and to mind thy own business, and thou wilt find that thou hast little leisure to take an inventory of another man's wealth.

XXIV

On Modern Philosophers

"Beware lest any man spoil you through philosophy and
vain deceit, after the tradition of men, after the rudiments
of the world."—*Coloss.* xi. 8.

IT was the lot and misfortune of St. Paul, in his various visits
to the cities of Greece, to hear and see a certain loquacious race of
sophists whom, by a nobler name than they deserved, he calls philosophers. Care must be taken not to confound these frontless bab-
blers with the wise men who flourished in an early era of the republic. The latter not only loved Wisdom but deserved and received all her favours; the former wore her livery, but were not
ranked even among her menials. The names of Socrates and Plato
will never be forgotten. The names of those metaphysical spiders
who covered the decayed edifice of the Grecian empire with their
filthy cobwebs, cannot easily be remembered.

From every passage where these sophists are mentioned in the
works of the apostle of Tarsus, it is clear that they were of the
same stamp, had the same stupid heads and the same bad hearts as
those of the moderns who, under the names of Paine, Condorcet,
Sieyes, and Marat, have "dashed and perplexed the maturest councils."

In an early age of my lay labours I believe I have already given
to this topic an honest and unprejudiced consideration. But the
rank poison of philosophy cannot be fully described in a single
column of a newspaper; and as, most unfortunately, some philosophers not only live but teach in America, it may be useful, in my
plain way, again to instruct my countrymen to beware of such
counterfeits.

These men, professing so much, are the veriest sciolists in nature. One might pertinently address one of these vain boasters in
the language of Job, "Canst thou bind the sweet influences of
Pleiades, or loose the bands of Orion? Canst thou bring forth
Mazzaroth in his season? or canst thou guide Arcturus with his
sons?"

A philosopher, in the modern sense of the word, I would define a presumptuous mortal, proudly spurning at old systems and promptly inventing new. Be the materials ever so naught, be their connexion ever so slight, be the whole ever so disjointed and crazy, if it be new, these confident architects will swear that their building will accommodate you better than any that you have previously used. To catch the eye and abuse the credulity of wondering fools, the puppet-show philosopher exhibits his scheme, gorgeously painted and gloriously illuminated, and bellows all the time in praise of his varnished ware. The whole is artfully calculated to captivate and charm all except those few who are not suddenly delighted with such representations, who know of what stuff they are made, for what purposes they are intended, and in what they are sure invariably to end. Such men gaze only to deride. But laugh as you please, the philosophers find in human nature such a fund of credulity that, be their draughts large as they may, no protest is anticipated. It is a bank, not merely of discount but deposit, and bolstered up by all the weakness in the world. The moment that a man arrives in this fairy and chivalric land of French philosophy he beholds at every creek and corner something to dazzle and surprise, but nothing steadfast or secure. The surface is slippery, and giants, and dwarfs, and wounded knights, and distressed damsels abound. Nor are enchanters wanting, and they are the philosophers themselves. They will, in a twinkling, conjure away kingdoms, chain a prince's daughter in a dungeon, and give to court-pages, to lacqueys, and all those "airy nothings," a local habitation and a name. If the adventurer in this fantastic region be capriciously weary of his old mansion, the philosophic enchanters will quickly furnish a choice of castles, "roughly rushing to the skies." They are unstable, it is true, and comfortless and cold and cemented with blood, but show speciously at a distance, with portcullis most invitingly open, for the free and equal admission of all mankind.

Those who have been professors of the new philosophy of France, and their servile devotees in America, taint every thing they touch; like the dead insect in the ointment, they cause the whole to send forth an odious and putrid savour. Instead of

viewing man as he is, they are continually forming plans for man
as he should be. Nothing established, nothing common is admitted into their systems. They invert all the rules of adaptation.
They wish to fashion nature and society in their whimsical
mould, instead of regulating that mould according to the propor-
tions of society and nature. They glow with intense love for the
whole species, but are cold and chill as death towards every individual. Condorcet wrote a kind of general epistle to the
churches which are in Africa. He was eager that the blacks of the
isles should be emancipated. Philosophy disdains the tardy step
of time and will not tell, even on her fingers, the digits of political and moral computation. Condorcet made clear work. A system is a talisman and worketh its wonders instantaneously. He
told every negro that could understand him to run from or kill
his master, and be free. *Nec mora;* nor was hesitation allowed;
the whole work might be finished in an hour. A Roman or Grecian projector, in the most lawless season of the ancient common-
wealths, would give some time to consideration and judge some
delay necessary for the ripening of his plans. A philosopher, like
a wizard, conjures quickly and calls at once all his hideous phantoms from the "vasty deep" of his depraved mind. Condorcet's
hope, unlike that of many of his visionary brethren, was lost in
fruition; and he had the satisfaction to behold the government of
St. Domingo administered by sable hands. To gain so useful an
end, the Frenchman was careless how many houses of the whites
were consumed, or how many bodies were butchered. Philosophy
instructed him that all men were equal, and to exalt a few slaves
to the height of their masters it was not necessary for his system to
show that infinite misery would ensue.—God forbid that I should
be once thought pressing an argument against the injured Africans.
I cordially wish they were all happy in their native land and im-
bibing all the sweets of their tropical fruit and their palmy wine.
But when they are once incorporated with us, even upon terms
unequal and oppressive, it is not a Condorcet that can make them
happy by riving the relation in an hour; it is not his philosophy
will mitigate a black man's woes, either in this life or in the life to
come.

[173]

To men of the complexon of Condorcet and his associates, most of the miseries of France may be ascribed. Full of paradox, recent from wire-drawing in the schools, and with mind all begrimed from the Cyclops cave of metaphysics, behold a Sieyes, in the form of a politician, drafting, *currente calamo* three hundred constitutions in a day, and not one of them fit for use, but delusive as a mountebank's bill and bloody as the habiliments of a Banquo.

Of this dangerous, deistical, and Utopian school, a great personage from Virginia is a favoured pupil. His Gallic masters stroke his head and pronounce him forward and promising. Those who sit in the same form, cheerfully and reverently allow him to be the head of his class. In allusion to the well marshalled words of a great orator, him they worship; him they emulate; his *Notes* they con over all the time they can spare from the "Aurora" of the morning, or French politics at night. The man has talents, but they are of a dangerous and delusive kind. He has read much and can write plausibly. He is a man of letters, and should be a retired one. His closet, and not the cabinet, is his place. In the first, he might harmlessly examine the teeth of a non-descript monster, the secretions of an African, or the almanac of Banneker. At home, he might catch a standard of weight from the droppings of his eaves, and seated in his epicurean chair, laugh at Moses and the prophets and wink against the beams of the Sun of Righteousness. At the seat of government, his abstract, inapplicable, metaphysico-politics are either nugatory or noxious. Besides, his principles relish so strongly of Paris and are seasoned with such a profusion of French garlic, that he offends the whole nation. Better for Americans that on their extended plains "thistles should grow, instead of wheat, and cockle, instead of barley" than that a philosopher should influence the councils of the country and that his admiration of the works of Voltaire and Helvetius should induce him to wish a closer connexion with Frenchmen. When a metaphysical and Gallic government obtains in America, may the pen drop from the hand, and "the arm fall from the shoulder blade" of the Lay Preacher.

XXV

Levity of the Age

"Whereunto shall I liken this generation? It is
like unto children."—*Matt.* xi. 16.

I challenge the rhetoricians to find an apter similitude to express the levity of the age.

The features of humanity vary with ever-varying time. Men are foxes at one season, tigers at another, and kittens or monkeys at a third. Sometimes, intent on grave affairs, we are a starched and solemn race, and sometimes we vacantly gambol with coral and go-cart.

The world has, by the fancy of bards or by the austerity of monks, been compared to a wilderness, to a prison, and to a madhouse. To me, its present aspect is a great nursery; the girls are busy in dressing dolls and the boys in playing at chuck-farthing or driving a hoop. All are frivolously employed; and into whatever nook I cast my eyes I see nothing but baby faces and childish play.

The occupations, the arts, the manners, and amusements of the age are all composed of the lightest materials. "Vive la bagatelle" is the general motto. The world now reminds me of an old wooden cut in the Scotch edition of my Bunyan. It is "Vanity Fair," and nothing prominent to be seen but Frenchmen, harlequins, mountebanks and dancing dogs.

I look into the memoirs of Sully and into the age of Louis XIV. I there read interesting narratives of an illustrious prince, magnanimous nobles, erudite clergy, and a gay people. I see arts, useful and splendid, displayed, and the artist wantoning in sunshine. I behold the great wheels of process turning, and, in every rotation, the important and the beneficial uppermost. I lay aside my books and look at modern Paris. It is like peeping into the show-box of the vagrant Savoyard. Everything shows fantastic and puerile. Legislators with bits of motley ribbon in their caps, and compelled to wear this republican girth-web, imagining themselves free. Prostitutes from the opera personating the soberest of our faculties; and chimney sweepers, not yet pure from their soot, laying their sable paws upon a constitution. Everywhere the tricks of scaramouch and the dialect of the gipsey. If I seek their chiefs I discover a monster with five heads, more whimsical than the he-goat of the prophet Daniel. If I would ask the day of the month, I hear the gibberish of Germinal and Pluviose, and courts of justice and a body of soldiers indicated by "revolutionary tribunal" and "expeditionary army."

But my eyes ache by gazing at these microscopic objects. Let us leave Paris and her great boys to blow bladders, or to drown cats and impale flies. We too are childish on this side of the Atlantic, though not quite so absurd or cruel in our sports as the French.

I am not at a loss in what class to rank an audience who snore over the scenes of Shakespeare and are broad awake to the mummery of pantomime. The fine gentleman or lady who can exchange a dollar for a curvet of Lailson's horses or the cup-and-ball necromancy of an Italian adventurer, appears to me as awkward as my nephew Bobby, now riding across my study on a broomstick.

Of all new faces, and of every exhibition, we are childish admirers. I have known a retainer to the British theatre, who there was scarcely permitted to snuff candles without a prompter, extolled by the rashness of American enthusiasm as another Henderson or Garrick.

In literature a childish taste prevails and childish effusions are the vogue. We suffer our ears to be smothered by tinkling epithets, and our understandings to be lullabied by the drowsy hum of opera. I have heard of those who have been infantine enough to go the sixth night to a tragedy whose only merit was the republican name of its hero, and who concluded a paper was classical and patriotic, of course, because its editor was an Irishman.

The apostle acknowledged that, in the early part of his life, he thought, spoke, and acted as a child; but when he took his degrees in the school of manhood he laid aside folly and her cap and bells. Though the piety of Saint Paul may be inimitable, yet his dignity and resolution may be copied. The Lay Preacher hopes that he shall no longer behold a large portion of full-grown fellow creatures sitting like children in the market place. Let us, therefore, in the quaint but meaning phrase of our Bible translators, "quit ourselves like men," and remember that we were formed for higher purposes than to pipe or to dance.

XXVI

On Restlessness

"And the gold of that land is good; there is bdellium and the onyx stone."—*Gen.* xi. 12.

MEN, ever eager in search of factitious joys, go down to the sea in ships, visit various and distant climes, and tempt evil in a thousand forms, when safe and cheap delight is to be procured at home. The merchant, says Horace, hurries to the Indies to secure a flight from poverty. A more reflecting adventurer, on the point of embarkation, might consider that poverty is alike discoverable in the east as the west, and might be as easily eluded at home as abroad. I consider few things more baneful than that species of discontent which urges to go here, and go there, rather than to persevere in an uniform conduct in a permanent station. Restlessness is ever a capital defect in character, generally indicating either a light mind or a tainted heart. The "foul fiend" is depicted as a wanderer, going to and fro and walking up and down. Cataline is described by Sallust, who saw him with a painter's eye, as ever tiring of things possessed and panting to reach the distant and the inaccessible. Hope presents the false light "gliding meteorous" before us; we follow, and are beguiled.

Then where, my dear countrymen, are you going, and why do you wander? "Oh! we are on the march to Georgia, and to Genessee, the genuine gardens of the Hesperides, exuberant in golden fruit. We are embarking for the Indies, expecting, under their hot sun, our fortunes will ripen in a year. Do not detain us with your dogmas. It is not advice we seek; it is gold."

If that be the motive of these long journeys from Dan to Beersheba, the time, trouble, and expense may be saved. Superfluous to ascend Potosi, when mines are under our feet. The field of industry is not remote; it is a kind of homestead, within reach and within view; and adventurers may believe that the gold of that land is good: there is bdellium and the onyx stone.

It has been so fashionable of late for gentlemen of Hartford, and others of a speculative turn, to argue the propriety of migrating to Georgia and to the lakes, that men look askance at domestic blessings and fancy that neither gold nor any thing else of value can be found, except among southern sands and at the foot of the falls of St. Anthony. But wealth and power are not bounded by geographical lines nor suddenly conjured from the earth by the instrument of a surveyor. A slower process is required, but it is sure. Labour and the plough effect more at home than twenty journeys abroad.

Suspend your schemes, ye speculators, and confide in the resources of your native soil. Refreshed by sweet and running waters, diversified by hill and valley, ventilated by buxom gales and fertilized by the kindest influence of heaven, America, quickened by industry, is the El Dorado of romance. From such a soil, tillage will derive gold, and the gold of that land is good where the yeoman is strenuous and persevering. Gazing at the full-eared corn, the ample hay-cock, and matured orchard, the rural enthusiast may exclaim: "*There* is bdellium and the onyx stone, the sources of our wealth and splendour."

XXVII

On Newsmongers

"For all the Athenians and strangers which were there, spent their time in nothing else, but either to tell or to hear some new thing."—Acts xvii. 21.

ATHENS, when visited by the apostle, was literally a barber's shop. The inhabitants, instead of examining the doctrines of the saints, asked only if they were *new*, without inquiring whether they were wholesome. Even the philosophers of the Areopagus, like the philosophers of France, were curious only of the fanciful and the strange, and left the true and the useful to the honest worshipper in the synagogue or the humble saunterer in the market-place. "What will this babbler say?" impatiently demanded the lounging epicurean and the captious stoic. Will he amuse us with tales of a fairy land of devotion, or will he interest us with a terrible and mysterious mythology of strange gods? Supine in the porticoes and temples of our city, we want something to ruffle or enchain the mind. Has the apostle travelled; has he taken a turn in the hanging gardens of Babylon or plunged into Roman baths; has he frolicked with the voluptuous Syrians or ascertained the altitude of the pyramids of Egypt; are the beauties of Corinth familiar to his memory, and has he heard the song of Persian bards? If he can narrate wonderful adventures, even the Diogenes of our tribe shall resign half his tub to the apostle. But if the good, the perfect, and the fair are the trite themes of his lecture, we will leave him "in the midst of Mar's hill" and inquire in the gymnasium how the last wrestling match concluded.

But we have been in Greece long enough. Athens is no more, and, recollecting an old adage, we will not insult her ashes. The busy curiosity of that city still survives, a kind of tutelary saint of every country. Though Solomon has protested against the search for novelty, men still ask "What news?" and the Quidnunc of Murphy's "Upholsterer" in every country reads gazettes, lingers in coffeehouses, haunts tea tables, and demands of politicians, barbers, and women, "the strange, the passing strange."

In America, the impertinent eagerness for news should be scolded or laughed into moderation. The country gentleman, at peace on his farm, asks for translations from the Paris *Moniteur,* absurdly anxious for the welfare of Frenchmen, skipping over the carcass of their king and country. Others are solicitous for the emperor Alexander and the grand Turk, and are not a little relieved to learn that the first traverses St. Petersburg at nine and that the last uses more opium than sherbet. I have known profound calculators so busy with Mr. Pitt and the Bank of England that they utterly neglected their own debts, and, proving a national bankruptcy abroad, were thoughtless of their own at home. One would suppose, from the general inquiries respecting European affairs, that Columbus had never discovered America; and that our interests, our hopes, and our fears grew in the streets of Paris and London or on the banks of the Rhine and Po.

In France, the "pleached bower" and the vines of the south have been forsaken, and men hurry to the *auberge* to inquire if the First Consul has ordained a new calendar or compiled a new constitution.

In Ireland the giddy sons of Ulster, instead of "uniting" to sow flax and urge the loom, have congregated tumultuously, studious of pernicious novelties. Desperate insurgents, dissatisfied with the old harp, pretended its string was too tense and its tone too bold, and wanted a new and vulgar instrument, grumbling, harsh and loud.

England, proverbial for its spirit of inquisitiveness, resembles a bumpkin, absurdly curious, asking what is this, what is that? Men lift the awful veil of the church and the curtain of the cabinet, not to venerate the ancient establishments but to ask bishop and king for new lawn and a new minister. Letters, as well as politics, are subjected to the rage for novelty. Shakspeare is rejected for flimsy farce and monstrous pantomime; for Hamlet is as old as the times of "Good Queen Bess," and the last dumb show was acted but yesterday.

Ye querists, ye quidnuncs, check your impertinent curiosity. Devote not life to hearing and telling new things. If ye have business, mind it; are you masters of families, stay at home. Your heads are too shallow to contain the myriads of novel ideas ye wish. Action, not tattle, is the business of life.

XXVIII

On Thanksgiving

"Give a sweet savour, and a memorial of fine flour: and make
a fat offering."—*Eccles.* xxxviii. 2.

YESTERDAY, as I was pondering a theme for my next discourse with an aching head which checked invention, my hair dresser entered my chamber with the daily papers in his hand. Men of his class being naturally fond of politics, anxious for the public weal, eager to ask and no less eager to tell the news, he therefore, after a few preliminary queries, informed me with an Englishman's pride that Sir Sidney Smith had destroyed the gunboats of the usurper and that the thunder of British cannon was rocking the whole coast of France. He uttered this in a tone so cheerful and with such sparkling eyes that for a moment, in spite of my rigid republicanism, I actually participated in his pleasure. While he was occupied in chattering with the volubility of his profession and in combing my grey locks, I picked up some of the papers and, as it behoved a preacher, looked for the grave and the moral. The politician and the man of the world will perhaps smile when I add that no articles so attached my attention as the proclamations for days of thanksgiving in some of the northern states. When I saw from every quarter the fairest evidences of autumnal plenty, I felt the propriety of devotional gratitude and was delighted that public commemoration of annual favours was one of the customs of my country.

In the most rude as well as refined ages, a lively perception of benefits conferred by Supreme Power has caused mankind to "give a sweet savour, and a memorial of fine flour, and to make a fat offering." Long before Christianity had shed its lustre on the nations, we find the Jew, the Roman, and the Greek raising the periodical hymn to the skies. Though their creeds, dictated by superstitious ignorance, were clashing and various, yet gratitude to the "giver" was one and the same. If a general had enlarged an empire by his enterprise or defended paternal fields with his gallantry; if "the sweet influences of a Pleiades" had graciously descended and Italian granaries burst with plenty, the grateful ancients decreed the festal day, and all orders, careless of business or pleasure, thronged the temples and thanked the Beneficent Power. Thanksgiving was one of the first acts of devotion described by the sacred historian. In the very infancy of time, amid the simplicity of pastoral life, we behold a striking scene: the amiable Abel, that blameless shepherd, selecting the fairest of the flock and sacrificing them on the first altar. From a social supper with his disciples, from crowds of penitent or plausive Jews, we find the Son of Mary retiring to the solitude of Mount Olivet, to render thanks that neither the persecuting Pharisee nor the subtle Sadducees had abridged his life or invalidated his doctrine. St. Paul, in his perilous voyage, when tossing in the Adriatic gulf and exposed to all the horrors of a nocturnal shipwreck, while he was wishing anxiously for day, did not employ the first moments of returning light in the cares of navigation but "gave thanks" for his safety and partook of bread and meat with the mariners.

But without recurring to ancient examples to fortify a duty in which there is so much pleasure to animate its exercise, I will now close by assigning a few reasons peculiarly binding on Americans for periodical gratitude.

While many nations of the elder world are convulsed by revolution, menaced with dangers, or groaning under servitude, we are leading "quiet and peaceable lives," and like the happy Sidonians, we dwell at once "careless and secure." No inquisitor summons our sectaries to the stake, and in no cell of America has the clank of religious chains yet been heard. No Turkish sultan abridges life by a nod, and no Lama of superstition tortures the credulity of ignorance or affronts the discernment of wisdom. Though Discord has hurled her brand among the nations, against the conflagration of war we have had the whole Atlantic as a ditch. The gleam of arms has only been contemplated in the distance, and the sound of European artillery has been as "thunder heard remote." Agonized France, under the mad domination of petty tyrants of the most execrable race enumerated in any of the rolls of history, has seen the lights of her church extinguished, her "nursing father" and "nursing mother" destroyed, her "nobles in fetters of iron" and her subjects ground between the upper and nether millstone of revolutionary experiment. The olive has yielded its oil to illumine the *lantern*, and the grape has been trodden by the faultering feet of the intoxicated soldier. Silent are the halls of the sovereign, and a Fox looks out of the window. Contrast this shaded picture, my countrymen, with the scenes of peace and plenty which environ you. Commerce wafts you her wares from afar and her merchandise from the ends of the earth. Husbandry has turned its furrow to vivifying air, and liberal harvests have been reaped from your fields; your oxen are "strong to labour," and your sheep scatter over the plains. Seeing, therefore, that you possess in tranquillity such a goodly heritage, be careful that charity go hand in hand with cheerfulness, and as you give thanks, give alms. To him who has no father, stretch the parental hand, and when "'the eye" of the begger "sees, then let it bless you." When you have thanked the great Giver and imparted from your store to him "that is ready to perish," then let the tabret sound in your feasts, then let the rejoicing heart rebound and the voice of gladness diffuse a general complacency.